JAMES BARNET

EXPLORING THE
NEVIS RANGE
AND MAMORES
SCOTLAND

JAMES BARNET

EXPLORING THE NEVIS RANGE AND MAMORES

SCOTLAND

MEREO

Cirencester

Mereo Books

1A The Wool Market Dyer Street Cirencester Gloucestershire GL7 2PR
An imprint of Memoirs Publishing www.mereobooks.com

Exploring the Nevis Range and Mamores, Scotland: 978-1-86151-247-5

First published in Great Britain in 2014
by Mereo Books, an imprint of Memoirs Publishing

Copyright ©2014

Cover design - Ray Lipscombe

The address for Memoirs Publishing Group Limited can be found at www.memoirspublishing.com

The Memoirs Publishing Group Ltd Reg. No. 7834348

The Memoirs Publishing Group supports both The Forest Stewardship Council® (FSC®) and the PEFC®
leading international forest-certification organisations. Our books carrying both the FSC label and the
PEFC® and are printed on FSC®-certified paper. FSC® is the only forest-certification scheme supported
by the leading environmental organisations including Greenpeace. Our paper procurement policy can
be found at www.memoirspublishing.com/environment

Typeset in 10.5/15pt Franklin Gothic
by Wiltshire Associates Publisher Services Ltd. Printed and bound in Great Britain
by Printondemand-Worldwide, Peterborough PE2 6XD

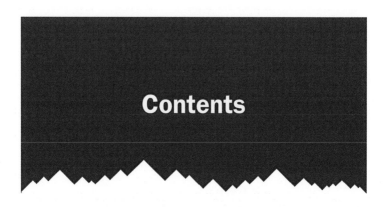

Contents

Introduction and scope of this book
About the author

THE PEAKS

INTRODUCTION TO THE ROUTES

Introduction and scope of this book

Ever since Sir Hugh Munro published his list of "Munro Tables" in 1891, these mountains have drawn increasing numbers of hill walkers to Scotland, with the aim of conquering them all and becoming "Munro-baggers". Sir Hugh Munro never actually climbed all of the Munros in his Tables himself, and the first "Munro-bagger" was Reverend A. E. Robertson in 1901. Since then, increasing numbers of "Munro-baggers" are added to the list each year.

Munros are mountains in Scotland whose summits rise greater than 3000ft (914.4m) above sea level, and believed to have sufficient elevation difference from adjacent summits to be considered as separate mountains. Mountain peaks which are of Munro height but not considered to be separate from an adjacent higher summit are called Munro Tops. Since the initial publication in 1891, there have been a number of revisions to the Munro Tables by the Scottish Mountaineering Club (SMC). In the latest 2012 revision, there are 282 Munros and 227 Munro Tops. Although Munros tend to grab many of the headlines amongst Scottish hill walkers, there are also interesting groups of mountains at <914.4m (<3000ft) in height that can provide an exciting challenge. Mountains between 914.4m and 762m (3000-

2500ft) with at least 152m (500ft) of descent on all sides are known as Corbetts, and mountains between 609.6m and 762m (2500-2000ft) with at least 152m (500ft) of descent on all sides are called Grahams. These hills are also receiving a recent revival in popularity.

The Fort William area in western Scotland, the self-acclaimed "outdoor capital of the UK", contains a particularly high density of Munros in the neighbouring Nevis and Mamore ranges. The Nevis Range is defined here as being bordered by the Great Glen to the north, Loch Linnhe to the west, Glen Nevis to the south and the valley of the Allt Coire an Eoin separating the Grey Corries to the east. The range is most famous for containing Ben Nevis, but it also comprises a further 3 Munros, 7 Munro Tops and two additional peaks of Graham height but with less than 152m of descent on all sides. Ben Nevis undoubtedly attracts more tourists than any other Munro in Scotland, due to its proximity to Fort William and stature as the highest in the British Isles. However the other Munros in the range all fall within the top 9 highest mountains in the country, and are included in a small elite group of summits that are >4000 feet in height.

The Mamore Range comprises an attractive group of mountains to the south of the Nevis Range, bordered by Glen Nevis to the north, Loch Linnhe to the west, Loch Leven to the south and Loch Eilde Mor to the east. Although the Munros are lower than those in the Nevis Range, they are linked by exciting ridges and can be combined to make some fantastic days out in the hills. The range comprises 10 Munros, a further 7 Munro Tops, 1 Corbett and a further two hills of Corbett height but with <152m of descent on all sides. The Mamores are far less frequented than the Nevis Range, but cover a larger geographic area and offer greater variety for the mountain explorer, with the potential for some very long multi-Munro bagging expeditions.

Many visitors to this area will just make one climb up Ben Nevis and claim they have been there, seen it and got the T-shirt (which can be bought in Fort William), but this book seeks to change that. Aiming to be the most complete guide for a hill walker exploring the Nevis and Mamore ranges, this book describes some of the best and most exciting routes across the area, ranging from peaceful strolls through scenic glens to ascents of the principal Munros and Munro Tops. All of the walks here have been tried and tested by the author, and are graded by a level of difficulty assuming some basic Munro climbing experience in Scotland. Each route is described in detail and accompanied by a sketch map, altitude profile and an abundance of photographs, so that the reader can better assess which routes are suitable for their fitness level, ability and desire. None of the walks included in this book require any specialist equipment (i.e. ropes, hard hats etc.) under good summer conditions, but many become serious mountaineering expeditions requiring specialist equipment and experience during the snow and ice of winter and spring. A detailed introductory chapter on the geological evolution of Scotland is included, so that the mountain walker can more fully appreciate the spectacular mountain scenery when out on an invigorating hill walk, and understand the geological processes that led to the formation of this beautiful landscape.

Mountain climbing anywhere in the world is a dangerous pursuit and fatalities occur on the Scottish Munros every year, typically peaking in winter. The popularity of the Fort William area throughout the year makes it a particular locus for fatal accidents. Practical advice and gear required for a mountain walk are therefore included, in an attempt to improve safety when out in these mountains.

The walks and circuits provided here are just suggestive, detailing the easiest and most interesting routes up the principal mountain summits in the Fort William area. This guide can therefore serve as an introduction for the experienced and adventurous who can fathom a seemingly endless variety of alternative exciting routes and circuits up these attractive and rewarding mountains.

About the author

James Barnet was born on 9 August 1986 in Southampton and grew up in the New Forest, Hampshire. He developed a strong understanding of geology from an early age, becoming a member of the Southampton Mineral and Fossil Society as well as Rockwatch (the club for young geologists), before subsequently obtaining a First Class Master's Degree in the subject from the University of Southampton. A particular highlight of his university education involved a field excursion to the Svalbard archipelago in the Barents Sea, to investigate palaeoclimate change during an extreme warming event that occurred around 55 million years ago and which may represent the closest geological analogue for present-day anthropogenic global warming.

In September 2008, James commenced full-time employment with an oil & gas consultancy near Oxford, with his geological travels taking him to contrasting parts of the world including Russia, Canada, Norway,

Oman and the USA. He also holds a keen interest in creative writing (winning a number of national writing competitions during his teenage years), botany (growing a number of rare and exotic plants in his garden in southern England), digital photography, meteorology, long-distance running and of course mountain climbing. This book, the culmination of over four years' work, builds on and unites many of those interests.

As his father hailed from Dundee, he used to travel up to Scotland regularly from an early age on family visits, mainly to Perthshire and eastern Scotland, but occasionally further afield to Skye or the Scottish west coast. James climbed his first Munro, Schiehallion, in August 2001, before visiting the Fort William area to climb Carn Mor Dearg on a hot summer's weekend in August 2004. After that trip James became hooked on the Munros in the Nevis and Mamore ranges, returning at least once every year, walking the routes he now lavishly describes in this book many times over. He now aims to broaden his Munro-climbing experience, tackling neighbouring summits further afield and one day hopes to add his name to the ever-growing list of "Munro baggers".

Disclaimer

This book is dedicated to my father (Douglas Barnet), mother (Shirley Barnet) and brother (Peter Barnet), who introduced me to this area in 2004 and accompanied me on many of the walks described in this book.

The Barnet family at the summit cairn on Carn Mor Dearg, July 2005

The geological evolution of Scotland and Great Britain

The formation of the impressive landscape around Fort William in western Scotland has been a long and complex one, commencing about 1,000 million years ago (Ma) during the Pre-Cambrian Period. During this time Scotland, along with the majority of Earth's continental blocks, formed part of a large supercontinent called Rodinia. Rifting of Rodinia commenced around 750 Ma, with the deposition of a thick succession of predominantly shallow marine sandstones, shales, limestones and volcanics within these rifts. These ancient marine sediments comprise the Dalradian Series, exposed across large tracts of the Grampian Highlands today. This rifting was followed by opening of the Iapetus Ocean from 600 Ma during the Late Pre-Cambrian. Rifting of the Iapetus Ocean severed the Baltica continent (comprising present-day Scandinavia, Eastern Europe and European Russia) and the Gondwana continent (comprising present-day Africa, South America, the eastern seaboard of North America, England, Wales and southern Ireland) away from the Laurentia continent (comprising North America, Greenland, Scotland and northern Ireland). Thus England and Scotland, once part of the same supercontinent, moved thousands of miles apart during the Late Pre-Cambrian (600-542 Ma) and subsequent Cambrian Period (542-488 Ma), as the vast Iapetus Ocean opened up between them. Deeper marine sediments started to accumulate around the margins of the Iapetus Ocean, forming the youngest sediments of the Dalradian Series in Scotland. Significantly different fossilised species of trilobites (an extinct marine organism resembling a large woodlouse) unearthed from Cambrian rocks in Scotland and Wales, emphasise the great separation that had developed between Gondwana and Laurentia by this time.

The Iapetus Ocean probably reached its widest extent during the Late Cambrian (about 510 Ma), when England and Scotland may have been 5000-7000 km apart. Both were located in the southern hemisphere, but while Scotland on the margin of Laurentia was situated at a low latitude of about 20°S, England and Wales on the margin of Gondwana were located at a high latitude of about 60°S. Rifting of the northern margin of Gondwana at about 500 Ma split away a northern fragment of the large continent comprising England, Wales, southern Ireland and the eastern seaboard of North America. This microcontinent, called Avalonia, commenced a long journey of northward movement towards Laurentia as a new ocean, the Rheic Ocean, opened up between Avalonia and Gondwana. Therefore by the end of the Cambrian (488 Ma), the Iapetus Ocean was bordered by Laurentia to the north and west, Baltica to the east and Avalonia to the south.

Many of the geological structures of the Scottish Highlands, along with the solid bedrock in the area covered by this book, represent the eroded core of a former mountain range of Himalayan proportions. This range spread west to form the ancestral Appalachian Range in North America, along with mountains in east Greenland, western Scandinavia (mainly Norway) and parts of central-eastern Europe. These mountains formed during several stages over a period of about 100 million years known as the

Caledonian Orogeny, representing the time from initial onset to final closure of the Iapetus Ocean. This started in the Late Cambrian, around 510 Ma, and lasted until the Mid-Late Silurian (430-410 Ma). The Caledonian Orogeny is represented by two main orogenic (mountain building) periods in Britain, the Grampian Orogeny during the Early-Middle Ordovician (480-460 Ma) and the Scandian Orogeny of Middle Silurian age (around 430 Ma).

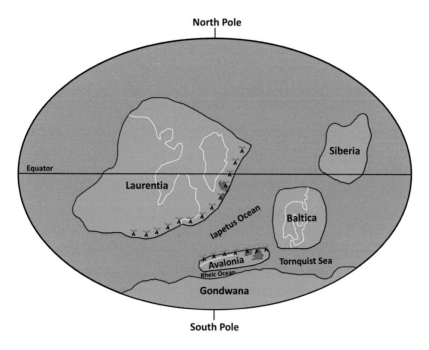

Global palaeogeography during the Middle Ordovician

During the Late Cambrian-Early Ordovician (510-485 Ma), the Iapetus Ocean started to rapidly close by subduction of oceanic crust beneath both its northern and southern margins. A volcanic range, much like the present-day Pacific Ring of Fire, sprang up across the northern margin of Avalonia and formed an island arc to the south of the Laurentian margin. This island arc, known as the Midland Valley Arc and now comprising the bedrock of the

Scottish Central Lowlands, subsequently collided with the Laurentian margin and marked the first phase of mountain building (Grampian Orogeny) across Scotland. Substantial metamorphism (burial and subjection to extreme heat and pressure) of the Dalradian sedimentary rocks took place, forming the solid metamorphic bedrock of the central-eastern Mamores and south-eastern Nevis Range. During the Late Ordovician (about 450 Ma), Avalonia collided with Baltica, and this new amalgamated continent continued to close in towards Laurentia.

The Iapetus Ocean finally closed during the Mid-Late Silurian (430-410 Ma), with the suturing of Avalonia and Baltica to Laurentia. The Iapetus Ocean zipped up from the north, with collision between Baltica and Laurentia occurring first, followed by collision of Avalonia. England and Scotland were united for the first time as part of a large continent called Laurussia, which also included North America, Greenland, Scandinavia, Eastern Europe and European Russia, separated from the large Gondwana continent by the Rheic Ocean. This final closure event initiated the final climax of the Caledonian Orogeny (Scandian Orogeny) during the Middle Silurian (430 Ma). It was at the end of this phase that the igneous rocks of the Nevis Range and western Mamores were intruded into the metamorphic Caledonian bedrock, the Caledonian mountain range reached Himalayan proportions, and Ben Nevis represented an active volcano. The predominant NE-SW structural grain of the metamorphic bedrock across Scotland reflects the orientation of the suture (collision zone) between Laurentia and Baltica/Avalonia, through which the igneous rocks of the area were subsequently intruded and erupted at the end of the collision phase. The position of this suture actually corresponds almost exactly to the boundary between England and Scotland today, so remarkably the boundary between the countries is not only political but geological.

Significant volumes of clastic sediment (composed of broken pieces of older rocks) were eroded from the Caledonian mountain

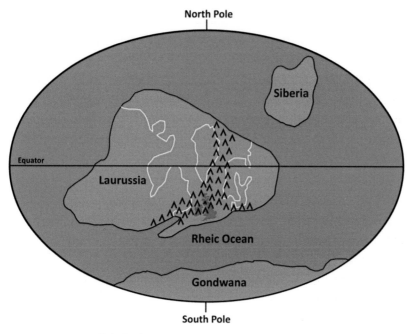

Global palaeogeography during the Early Devonian

range during the subsequent Devonian period (410-360 Ma). These conglomerates and sandstones were deposited in a range of continental environments, including intermontane lake basins, floodplains and alluvial plains, to form the Old Red Sandstone Formation. By the end of the Devonian, rapid denudation is believed to have significantly reduced the elevation of the Himalayan-scale Caledonian mountain range.

A warm tropical sea spread across and around the remnants of the Devonian mountain range during the Carboniferous period (360-300 Ma), extending from the closing Rheic Ocean to the south. Volcanism continued across parts of Scotland during the Carboniferous, forming the famous Arthur's Seat near Edinburgh; however no further volcanism returned to the Nevis Range or Mamores.

At the end of the Carboniferous the Rheic Ocean closed, and all of the Earth's continental blocks amalgamated to form a massive supercontinent called Pangaea. This supercontinent was surrounded by an enormous ocean known as Panthalassa. A large marine gulf extending towards the centre of Pangaea opened up, called the Tethys Ocean. This collision resulted in the Variscan Orogeny (also known as the Hercynian Orogeny), once again uplifting the Appalachians in eastern North America, the Pyrenees along the French/Spanish border and the Urals along the Europe/Asia border. No major orogeny occurred in Britain, further away from the continental suture zone, although uplift occurred across the whole country. Intense metamorphism from this event only occurred across south-west England, closest to the suture with Gondwana, forming the famous building slates of Cornwall.

The granite plutons of Devon and Cornwall were also intruded during this time, including those on Dartmoor, Bodmin Moor and Land's End: these are small solidified buoyant tongues from a large underlying body of molten rock known as the Cornubian Batholith.

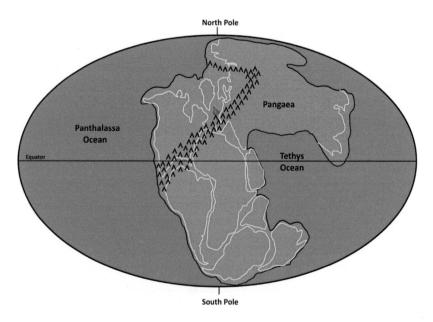

Global palaeogeography at the end of the Carboniferous Period

The hot desert of Oman, an analogue for how the landscape of Scotland
may have looked like during the Permian-Triassic periods

A harsh desert climate developed across Scotland during the
Permian and Triassic periods (299-200 Ma). During this time the
country was in the heart of the Pangaea Supercontinent, drifting
slowly northward through low northern latitudes to reach about
30°N by the end of the Triassic. Continental coarse-grained
conglomerates and sandstones accumulated across western
Scotland to form the New Red Sandstone Formation, deposited in
desert sand dunes, wadis and evaporative playa lakes, comparable
to that of the Sahara Desert, Namib Desert or Middle East today.
The New Red Sandstone is mainly preserved across south-west
Scotland and some Scottish islands such as Mull and Lewis. A
restricted epicontinental sea formed in the European Permian
Basin across eastern Britain, the North Sea, Germany and Poland
during the Late Permian (270-250 Ma), in which thick halite (salt)
deposits of the Zechstein Formation were deposited under the hot
and arid climate.

The break-up of Pangaea occurred during Jurassic-Cretaceous times (200-65 Ma), with the opening of the Atlantic Ocean to the west of Britain, the consequent rifting away of the Americas from Europe and Africa, and rifting of the North Sea Graben as a failed rift system to the east of Britain. No sediments of this age have been discovered across the Nevis and Mamore area; however marine shales and limestones were deposited fairly widely during these periods across the globe, times of high atmospheric CO_2 levels, very warm humid climates and high eustatic sea level. Fossiliferous marine shales, limestones and sandstones of Jurassic age have been extensively studied on the Isle of Skye and Raasay to the west, with scattered outcrops of Cretaceous sandstones and limestones discovered on the Hebridean islands, confirming that marine basins did certainly exist in fairly close proximity to this area. The northward movement of Britain continued and by the end of the Cretaceous period, at the point of extinction of the dinosaurs, Scotland was located at about 45°N. The country therefore moved a further 10°N during the course of the Cenozoic Era, from 65 Ma to present.

Major doming and uplift, associated with the opening of the North Atlantic and intrusion of the North Atlantic Tertiary Igneous Province above a mantle plume, affected western Scotland during the latest Cretaceous and Cenozoic. Pre-existing Caledonian structures were reactivated and a highland was initiated across north-western and central Scotland once more. This was accompanied by a significant volume of volcanic activity during the Palaeocene epoch (about 62-55 Ma), with extrusion of basaltic lavas forming the impressive volcanic landscapes across Skye, Mull and Eigg, such as the Old Man of Storr. The eroded gabbroic magma chambers of these volcanoes are now exposed in the spectacular Black Cuillin Range on Skye. This volcanic activity initiated a tilting of Britain towards the south-east, therefore whilst north-western Britain was being uplifted during the early Cenozoic, subsidence

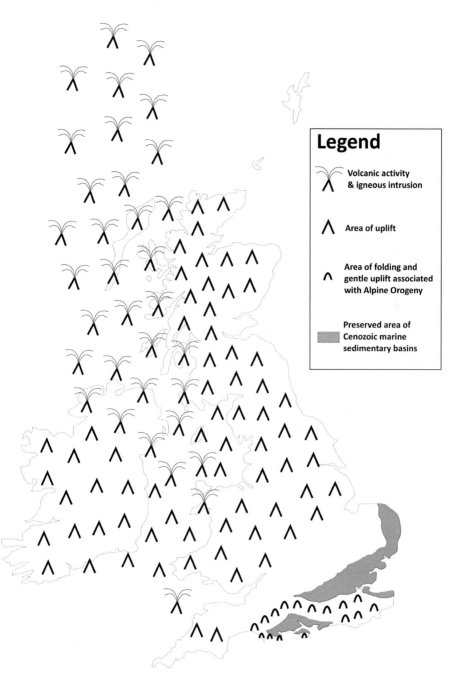

Palaeogeography of the British Isles during the early Cenozoic

took place across SE England, with deposition of fossiliferous marine sediments during the late Palaeocene, Eocene and Oligocene epochs (about 56-23 Ma). Closure of the Tethys Ocean during the middle of the Cenozoic (around 40-20 Ma) resulted in the collision of Africa with Europe and development of the Alpine Orogeny, creating extensive folding and uplift of the Alps and the Pyrenees in central Europe. In Britain, Alpine deformation, magnified by compression associated with opening of the North Atlantic Ocean to the west, was most pronounced in southern England closest to the collisional suture. Hills and structures such as the Purbecks, the central backbone of the Isle of Wight and the Weald-Artois Anticline were formed during this time.

The final important phase in the shaping of Scotland's present-day topography was at least three phases of widespread glaciation (Anglian, Wolstonian and Devensian), which have sculpted and shaped this mountain range for at least the past 300,000 years. Since Scotland was a highland from the early Cenozoic, and may have been uplifted again during the Pliocene epoch (5-2 Ma), glaciation of this higher topography may have started significantly earlier (as much as 2.5 million years ago). These glacial episodes were separated by interglacial periods, when the ice melted and the climate was comparable to or often warmer than that of today.

The oldest evidence of Cenozoic glaciation on Earth comes from Antarctica, which has occupied a position close to the South Pole for at least the past 100 million years. A permanent ice cap had grown to cover this large polar continent by the Eocene/Oligocene boundary around 34 Ma, following the opening of the Drake Passage and the development of a circumpolar ocean current allowing the "thermal isolation" of Antarctica. This rapid continental ice sheet growth initiated a major eustatic marine regression (sea level fall), correlated in marine sediment successions across the globe. Declining atmospheric CO_2 levels played a significant role in the transition from early Cenozoic "greenhouse" climates during the

Palaeocene and Eocene epochs (65-34 Ma), when CO_2 levels were high above present-day levels, to middle-late Cenozoic "icehouse" conditions and progressive cooling since the Oligocene epoch. Glaciation of Greenland, the second largest continental ice cap on Earth, took place during an abrupt cooling phase at the start of the Middle Miocene about 16 million years ago, followed by a progressive expansion of ice across the landmasses of the northern hemisphere.

The past three glacial-interglacial cycles appear to have a fairly well defined cyclicity, covering a 100,000 year (100 kyr) timespan. These cycles have been explained by a form of orbital forcing known as eccentricity. The orbit of the Earth around the Sun is not circular but elliptical, and its eccentricity describes how elliptical this orbit is (i.e. how much it differs from that of a perfect circle). The variations in the Earth's orbit were described by the Serbian astronomer and geophysicist Milutin Milankovic. Over time, the orbit of the Earth around the Sun changes from becoming more elliptical (high eccentricity) to more circular and less elliptical (low eccentricity), with the timescale of a full cycle from one state to the other and back again lasting 100,000 years. The point when the Earth is closest to the sun is known as perihelion, and that when it is furthest from the sun aphelion.

It has been proven that the critical factor controlling the onset of permanent glaciation is summer warmth. If summers are hot, more glacial snow and ice melts than can be replaced during the subsequent winter. Therefore, during an orbit with high eccentricity, the Earth passes closer to the sun during perihelion and summers would be warmer with a greater seasonal contrast than during a low eccentricity orbit, all other factors being equal. Consequently, the major glaciations have broadly corresponded to episodes of low eccentricity, when the Earth's orbit is closer to being circular, summer temperatures are cooler with reduced melting of snow and ice, and seasonal contrast is less. Other factors do come into play though and longer scale eccentricity cycles are also modulated by precession (a switch in the direction of tilt of the Earth's axis with a timescale of 21,000 years), and obliquity (changes in the angle of tilt of the Earth's axis with a timescale of 41,000 years), which serve to amplify or reduce the severity of seasonal contrasts and glaciations on shorter timescales. Interestingly, Earth's orbit is currently in a low eccentricity state, which means that the climate should be cooling and the onset of glaciation approaching. The fact that global temperatures during the past few hundred years (a period sometimes termed the "Anthropocene") have been rising, is one of many arguments in favour of anthropogenic global warming.

The last of these widespread glaciations, the Devensian, reached its peak about 23-21,000 years ago (23-21 Ka), when permanent ice sheets spread as far south as South Wales, the Midlands, and even close to the Isles of Scilly. This ice is believed to have largely disappeared by 15 Ka; however it did return for a final time to Scotland around 13 Ka, to provide a final modification to the glacial scenery across the Nevis Range and Mamores before entering our current interglacial period. The locking up of vast volumes of water in huge continental ice sheets in the high latitudes initiated a eustatic sea level fall on the order of 100m, subaerially exposing large portions of the North Sea and English Channel shelves. Interestingly, flooding of the eastern English Channel and southern North Sea did not take place until a few thousand years ago, so only very recently (in geological terms) have the islands of Great Britain become isolated from continental Europe.

During the height of the glaciations, western Scotland was buried beneath as much as 2,000m of ice, with the thickest ice sheet located across what is now the site of Britain's largest bog, Rannoch Moor. Thus many of the Munro summits would have been buried beneath the ice during maximum glaciation, or poking through the ice sheet as rocky "nunataks". Sculpting of the peaks therefore mainly occurred early and late in the glacial phase, with each successive major glaciation overprinting and destroying evidence of the former. Evidence of this glaciation is widespread throughout the area, including attractive U-shaped valleys, narrow rocky arêtes, and intricately scoured mountain corries. Coire Giubhsachan between the Carn Mor Dearg Arête and the Aonach Beag Massif is a particularly spectacular example, with remains of the glacial moraine and striated erratic boulders still preserved at the lower end of the valley, where the foot of the former mountain glacier was once located.

The glacial scouring of corries and U-shaped valleys in action, Svalbard

13

Terminal moraine and erratic boulders at the foot of Coire Giubhsachan

Erosion of the Scottish Highlands continues at the present day, with the combined effects of wind, rain, ice and snow continuing to weather away the crystalline core of the Caledonian mountain range. Perhaps in many millions of years' time this will once again reduce the range to sea level.

The geology of the Nevis and Mamore ranges

The rock record in the Nevis Range and Mamores mainly comprises igneous and metamorphic rocks formed before, during or immediately after the Caledonian Orogeny. These rocks are >400 million years old, some significantly so. Whilst younger sediments may have been deposited here (such as the New Red Sandstone or marine sediments of Cretaceous age), they have not been preserved, due to Cenozoic uplift and subsequent glaciation.

Igneous rocks form from the crystallisation of magma slowly underground (intrusive igneous rocks) or from the more rapid cooling of lava at the Earth's surface (extrusive igneous rocks). Metamorphic rocks form from the burial of a sedimentary protolith (sandstone, limestone or shale), and transformation deep underground by high temperatures and/or extreme pressures into a new rock type stable at such extreme Pressure-Temperature (P-T) conditions. This commonly involves the dissolution of mineral phases and precipitation as a new stable form, often as distinct veins within the rock or as a new crystal lattice. Once exhumed at the surface, such rocks are no longer in equilibrium with the surface P-T conditions and are geochemically "metastable", requiring some form of activation energy (either heat or pressure) before the transformation process into a new stable mineral form can take place.

Three different grades of metamorphism are noted by geologists, from low through medium to high-grade, to describe increasing P-T conditions that the rock has experienced from the former to the latter. Metamorphism does not exceed medium grade across the area covered by this book, except in the far south-east of the area (around Loch Eilde Mor) and the north-west around Fort William, Cow Hill and Loch Linnhe. High-grade metamorphic rocks are also described from the north-west of Scotland and the Outer Hebrides, where the ancient rocks may have been subjected to multiple phases of metamorphism (polymetamorphism). Unknown to many people, diamonds are also metastable at the Earth's surface, having been formed deep underground under high P-T conditions in kimberlite pipes. Fortunately, it is unlikely that this will affect your diamond jewellery.

Several different types of igneous and metamorphic rocks comprise the bedrock of the Nevis and Mamore ranges, and the abundant rock exposure at the exposed summits allows for a good examination of each.

Igneous rocks

Igneous rocks within the area were erupted or intruded at the end of the Caledonian Orogeny (around 420-410 Ma). These rocks include:

■ Pink or red **granite**, a coarse-grained intrusive igneous rock of felsic composition, composed predominantly of clear quartz, white plagioclase feldspar, pink or red potassium feldspar (giving the rock its distinctive colour), and black flakes of biotite mica. Granite offers good grip to the walker or ridge wanderer, being mainly distributed across the summits of the Nevis Range (with the exception of the central core of the Ben Nevis Massif and Aonach Beag), along with Mullach nan Coirean and Meall a' Chaorainn in the western Mamores. Further afield, large granite complexes of similar age are also found around Glen Coe, Glen Etive and across Rannoch Moor. The Nevis Range is actually composed of two distinct granite complexes: a coarser grained Outer Granite (comprising the bedrock of Aonach Mor) and a finer grained Inner Granite, which was intruded later and makes up Carn Mor Dearg.

■ Pale to dark grey **andesite**, a medium-grained extrusive igneous rock of intermediate composition, composed predominantly of white-grey plagioclase feldspar, dark grey-green pyroxene and hornblende. Andesite comprises the central core of the Ben Nevis Massif, including the summit itself and its north-west Top Carn Dearg. The andesitic lavas of Ben Nevis subsided into the molten granite now comprising Carn Mor Dearg and Aonach Mor following collapse of a solid block of schist comprising the cauldron roof, a process known as "cauldron subsidence".

Inner Granite with euhedral quartz crystals and veins, Carn Mor Dearg

Metamorphic rocks

Metamorphic rocks within the area belong to the Appin Group of the Dalradian Series and were

Andesite scree, Ben Nevis

laid down across the Rodinia Supercontinent during the Late Pre-Cambrian Period (750-600 Ma). Sandstones, shales and limestones were initially deposited in rift basins, before being subsequently metamorphosed during the Grampian phase of the Caledonian Orogeny (480-460 Ma). These metamorphic rocks include:

▪ Pale grey-white **quartzite**, composed almost entirely of quartz, the metamorphic product of a quartz-rich sandstone protolith. Quartzite is a hard rock tending to fracture to form rough scree with sharp edges, which attack the walking boots and take no prisoners for anyone unfortunate enough to fall over on it. Quartzite is mainly distributed across the summits of the Mamores, alternating with schist as far west as Stob Ban, but also comprises the pointed summit of Sgurr a' Bhuic to the south of Aonach Beag. Large

18

exposures of bright white quartzite across the summits of Stob Ban, Sgurr a' Mhaim and Sgurr a' Bhuic look conspicuously like snow in certain lights. This attractive rock can take on an orange or pink hue if trace impurities such as iron are present.

■ Grey **schist**, a medium-grade metamorphic rock, the metamorphic product of a mud or shale protolith, is composed predominantly of platy grains of mica, chlorite, hornblende and graphite. These platy minerals are preferentially aligned parallel to each other to form a foliation, the result of formation under intense pressure due to deep burial associated with crustal thickening and orogenesis. Often this foliation is intensely deformed into numerous parasitic folds, which can be particularly well examined in the Nevis Gorge. Quartz, dissolved during metamorphism, is often precipitated as distinctive veins within the schist. This medium-grade metamorphic rock offers fairly good grip to the walker, but tends to fracture to tabular or platy blocks and scree across the Munro summits. Ridges composed of a schistose bedrock are often covered in grass, such as the Devil's Ridge between Sgurr an lubhair and Sgurr a' Mhaim. Schist, along with quartzite, is distributed across many of the summits of the central-eastern Mamores, along with the summits of Aonach Beag and Stob Coire Bhealaich in the south-eastern Nevis Range.

Quartzite, Stob Ban

■ Grey **gneiss**, a high-grade metamorphic rock, only distributed in the south-eastern extremity of the region south-east of Sgurr

Slabs of schist wedged in mud, Aonach Beag summit plateau

Eilde Mor, and in the north-west around Fort William and Loch Linnhe. The foliation within the rock is often intensely deformed into parasitic folds.

■ Black or grey **slate**, a low-grade metamorphic rock, the metamorphic product of a mud or shale protolith, composed predominantly of quartz and micas. This rock forms low hills to the west of Ben Nevis and Mullach nan Coirean.

The only sedimentary rocks exposed in the area, with the exception of Quaternary glaciogenic deposits and alluvium developed around present-day rivers, are the Ballachulish limestones. These limestones, still part of the Dalradian Series, do not appear to have been subjected to sufficient heat and pressure to be transformed into marble. These carbonate rocks are mainly distributed with low-grade metamorphic slates to the west of Ben

20

Nevis and Mullach nan Coirean, where they have been metamorphosed to a very hard rock called hornfels close to the contact with younger igneous intrusions.

A schematic geological map across the area (courtesy of BGS) is presented below, illustrating clearly how the igneous rocks of the Nevis Range and western Mamores were intruded through, and cross cut, the prevailing NE-SW structural grain of the metamorphic bedrock.

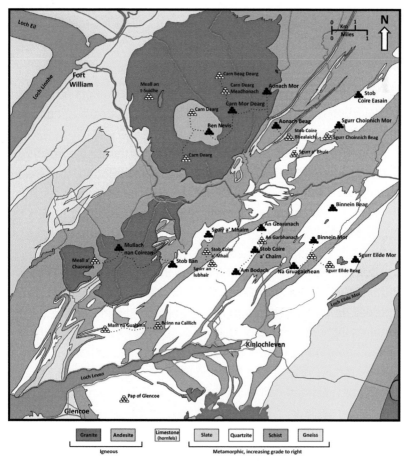

Geological map of the walking area (Courtesy of BGS)

The history of Ben Nevis

No book on this area would be complete without a short account of the interesting history of Ben Nevis, Britain's highest, most popular and best-known mountain.

The first recorded ascent of Ben Nevis, at the time considered but not confirmed to be the highest mountain in Britain, was made by a botanist from Edinburgh called James Robertson on 17 August 1771. This was quickly followed by a second recorded ascent in 1774 by geologist John Williams, to assess the mountain's potential for economic mineral deposits.

Ben Nevis was finally confirmed as the highest mountain in the British Isles by the Ordnance Survey in 1847, creating a flurry of interest, in particular regarding weather conditions at the top of Britain's highest mountain. To investigate this further, a gentleman by the name of Clement Lindley Wragge from Fort William climbed the mountain daily during the summer and autumn of 1881 and 1882, to make meteorological observations at the summit. Clement Wragge struggled up the mountain every day despite periods of atrocious weather, acquiring the informal nickname of "inclement Wragge". His work was considered extremely valuable by the

Scottish Meteorological Society however, and resulted in the construction of a permanently-staffed weather observatory at the summit in the summer of 1883, to allow 24-hour monitoring of the weather conditions.

A proper track to the summit of the mountain was constructed for the first time by a contractor called James McLean of Fort William, so that provisions could be delivered to the observatory, mainly by pony back. This is still the most popular route up Ben Nevis today, where it is commonly known as the "Mountain Track" but also informally as the "Tourist Track" or "Pony Track". Only over the past few years has the path been upgraded since its original construction in 1883, to cope with the huge volume of walkers (estimated at >100,000) who use the track each year.

The Ben Nevis observatory was finally opened on 17 October 1883 and recorded hourly observations at the summit for 21 years, until it was closed due to a lack of government funding in 1904. Two observers and a cook were in residence at the observatory, taking meteorological measurements such as air pressure, temperature, wind speed, rainfall and snow depth. Record sheets were taken down on foot to the Superintendent's House, now known as the Glentower Lower Observatory Guesthouse on the eastern shore of Loch Linnhe, by the mailman via the Mountain Track once a week during summer. The residents of the observatory had to cope with some extraordinary weather, including being buried beneath metres of snow and battling with winds well in excess of 100mph. The observatory was almost destroyed by lightning in 1895. The residents were essentially cut off from Fort William for many months during the winter and spring, as snow and ice covered the Mountain Track and delivery of provisions by pony back was impossible. The observations made during this time are the most complete for any mountain summit in Scotland, and provide valuable data to contrast with weather records from Fort William, close to sea level.

Coinciding with the construction of the West Highland Railway to Fort William and a consequent increase in tourism within the region, the Temperance Hotel was constructed at the summit of Ben Nevis around 1894. This hotel, attached to the meteorological observatory and constructed out of wood, consisted of four rooms costing 10 shillings each per night and also served breakfast, lunch and dinner. At the same time, the observatory building was expanded with the addition of a tower to rise above the deep winter snows, which had often prevented observatory residents escaping from the building to take measurements during winter storms. A prominent emergency shelter sits atop the ruins of this tower today, a useful refuge during ferocious weather on the mountain.

Once the observatory closed down, the hotel also took over the old observatory building and continued to serve refreshments until around 1916. The buildings of both the hotel and observatory have become ruins and distinctive landmarks across the otherwise featureless summit plateau of the Ben since the 1950s, following a major fire in 1932 and subsequent theft of the remaining lead from the observatory roof.

Ever since the construction of the Mountain Track, mankind has tried to find more and more diverse ways of reaching the summit. The first evidence of hill running on Ben Nevis was recorded during 1895, and the first competitive race featuring 10 competitors was held in June 1898. These races continued until 1903, then recommenced again from 1937 until the present day. This race now takes place on the first Saturday of September and is restricted to 600 competitors, starting and finishing at the Claggan Park football ground in Fort William. The record was set in 1984 by Kenny Stuart, who completed the course up and down the mountain in 1 hour and 25 minutes, an incredible time considering it takes the average walker about 7 hours to climb and descend the mountain via the Mountain Track from Glen Nevis. Ben Nevis' North Face first attracted the attention of climbers late in the 19th century, with the first recorded descent of Tower Ridge made in 1892, soon followed by an ascent in 1894. The now infamous rock and ice climbing routes up the North Face have subsequently become popular pursuits since the late 1930s.

Meanwhile, the arrival of the 20th century saw the transport of various peculiar objects up the Mountain Track to the summit of the mountain. In 1911, Henry Alexander (a motorist from Edinburgh) incredibly drove a Model T Ford up the Mountain Track to the summit of Ben Nevis, to demonstrate the versatility of the car. A piano was unearthed from beneath a cairn at the summit in 2006, allegedly carried up by a group of removal men from Dundee 20 years earlier. Other items to make it to the top of Ben Nevis include a bed, unicycles, an organ, a wheelbarrow and a barrel of beer. No other mountain in Scotland can boast such an array of peculiarities.

The final stage in the history of Ben Nevis was a purchase of the mountain and adjacent area, including Carn Mor Dearg, Aonach Beag and the northern half of Glen Nevis as far east as Sgurr Choinnich Beag, by the John Muir Trust in 2000. This charity aims to manage the ecology of the area by removing sheep from the wild mountain slopes and reducing deer populations, along with minimising the anthropogenic impact on the natural environment resulting from the passage of over 100,000 tourists a year. Staff and volunteers of the trust help to maintain footpaths, clear up litter, and destroy meaningless cairns which could pose navigational hazards during poor visibility. With the increasing popularity of this area for recreational activities, the good work of the John Muir Trust is vital to preserve this beautiful landscape for future generations to enjoy.

Weather and climate

The climate of the Fort William area is often described by the layman as "mild and wet", or more accurately by meteorologists as "temperate maritime", characterised by prevailing moist westerly winds from the neighbouring Atlantic Ocean. Mean climate data for the nearest official weather station to Fort William (Tulloch Bridge) and the Aonach Mor Ski Centre is presented on the next few pages, and compared to data from Edinburgh on the east coast of Scotland and London in south-east England. These graphs and the comparisons between them highlight the most important points about the climate of the Fort William area:

■ The area receives >2.5 times the average annual rainfall of Edinburgh and >3 times that of London.

■ London has 54% and Edinburgh 62% of the average number of rain days (defined as days where greater than 1mm of rainfall is recorded) per year in Fort William.

■ The sunniest and driest weather typically occurs on average during spring and early summer in Fort William, however each year is highly variable and pleasant weather can occur at other times of the year.

■ Data from the Ben Nevis summit meteorological observatory, obtained from 1883-1904, suggests that the summit plateau of Ben Nevis receives about 5 times the average annual rainfall of Fort William and has a mean annual temperature of just below 0°C.

The weather in Lochaber is extremely fickle and a proper consultation of the weather forecast before leaving home and daily once in the area is required, in order to formulate a plan for the best activities to do each day. In general, both local and national weather forecasts broadcast on the television or radio are useful as a starting point but insufficient for the mountain explorer, tending to focus on meteorological conditions in the major towns and cities or at low elevations around the sites of major human habitation.

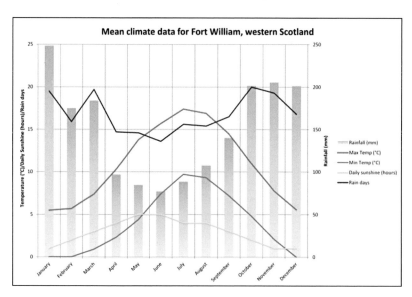

Mean climate data from Tulloch Bridge, 32km (20 miles) ENE of Fort William (Contains public sector information licensed under the Open Government Licence v1.0)

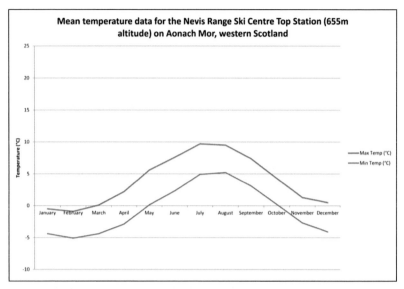

Mean temperature data from the Nevis Range Ski Centre Top Station, 655m altitude on Aonach Mor (Contains public sector information licensed under the Open Government Licence v1.0)

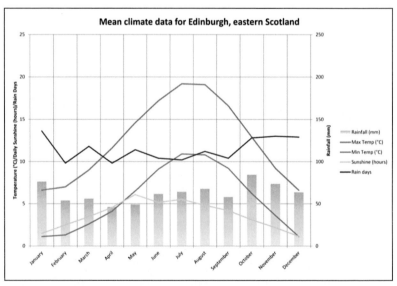

Mean climate data from Edinburgh, eastern Scotland (Contains public sector information licensed under the Open Government Licence v1.0)

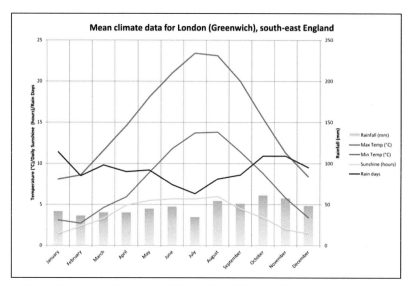

Mean climate data from London (Greenwich), SE England (Contains public sector information licensed under the Open Government Licence v1.0)

Mountain forecasts for Scotland are issued twice daily by the Met Office and are divided into two areas, West Highland and East Highland, with all mountains described in this book slotting comfortably into the West Highland forecast area. These forecasts cover the next five days; however accuracy tends to tail off towards the latter parts of the forecast, especially during unsettled weather patterns. These forecasts cover all aspects of mountain weather essential to walkers, including:

- A brief summary of general weather conditions expected across the forecast area, along with any changes likely to take place during the day.

- A summary of the risk of predicted weather hazards including: blizzards and heavy snow, gale, severe gale or storm force winds, dense and persistent hill fog, heavy rain or thunderstorms, wind chill and strong sunshine.

- General visibility across the area, beneath the cloud base.
- Altitude of the cloud base and extensiveness of hill fog predicted, along with changes expected during the day.
- Maximum wind speeds above 600m and maximum temperatures expected in the glens and at 900m altitude (near base Munro height).
- Elevation of the freezing level (0°C isotherm) if below the height of the highest Munros (which can occur even during midsummer).

As interest has increased in climbing the Scottish Munros during recent years, these forecasts have become readily available through an increasing range of broadcasting media, including:

- The Met Office website (www.metoffice.gov.uk).
- A useful free smartphone app called "Mountain Info Service".

They are also available from many businesses and tourist centres in Fort William, including:

- The entrance to Nevisport, at the Parade end of the main High Street.
- In the Glen Nevis Visitor Centre next to the main car park for the Mountain Track up Ben Nevis.
- In many major campsites and youth hostels in Fort William and the surrounding area.

Although the accuracy of short-range weather forecasting has improved substantially in recent years, predicting the weather across planet Earth is still an inexact science. In mountainous areas such as this, unpredicted and sudden weather changes can, and too often do, occur. Therefore it is important to always carry suitable clothing for cold/wet weather even if the weather forecast suggests a mainly warm and sunny day is ahead.

Keeping an eye on the rainfall radar when out and about in the mountains can provide an early warning of incoming unpredicted rainfall (or other precipitation), and can be accessed from www.meteox.com on a mobile with sufficient network coverage, which is often unreliable away from the centre of Fort William or Munro summits. Rain showers have an annoying and nasty habit of suddenly developing over high mountains such as Ben Nevis in the heat of the day, however. Under such changeable conditions, looking up into the sky and monitoring cloud development may prove to be a better means of forecasting than any high-tech equipment. The sudden development of low or convectively-rising cloud, along with an abrupt lowering of the cloud base and a freshening wind, may all be indicative of a developing shower or incoming band of rain.

A basic understanding of meteorology can often prove useful when planning a trip to the Scottish Highlands to coincide with a settled spell of weather. Of course, whether hill fog blankets the tops of the Munros depends on many factors beyond the scope of the amateur meteorologist, but a basic consideration of surface air pressure, wind direction and temperature can play a significant role in deciding if conditions are likely to be good in the mountains.

Four schematic surface pressure charts for the UK are illustrated over the next few pages, and arranged in order of the most favourable pressure set-ups for prolonged good weather in the West Highlands, along with the typical weather conditions expected and when in the year these are most likely to occur.

Such surface pressure charts, updated daily, can be accessed for free from www.metoffice.gov.uk.

Scandinavian High Set-up

■ High pressure centred over Scandinavia ("Scandi High"), with low pressure to the south-west of Britain, drags in a south-easterly airstream across the West Highlands.

■ The Scandi High "blocks" the normal eastward passage of Atlantic depressions across northern Britain, often resulting in prolonged settled weather in western Scotland, with the greatest chance of unsettled weather across south-western Britain.

■ The continental air mass, having travelled across continental Europe and the length of the UK, is very dry, resulting in prolonged sunshine and little or no hill fog.

■ Typically produces cold, sunny weather during winter and hot sunshine in summer.

■ Visibility is often good or excellent during the cold winter or early spring months, but may be only moderate during summer heat waves.

■ Most common during March-June.

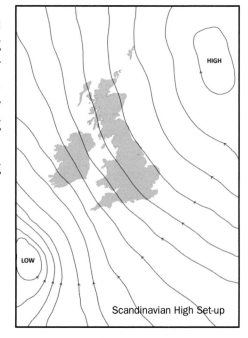

Scandinavian High Set-up

Arctic High Set-up

- High pressure centred to the north of the UK or across Greenland, with low pressure to the south-east of Britain, results in an easterly or north-easterly airstream across Scotland.

- The easterly winds tend to blow showers off the North Sea into eastern Scotland, whereas these showers often fizzle out before reaching the sheltered Western Highlands.

- Typically produces cold or cool weather conditions. Across the Western Highlands, prolonged sunshine with excellent air clarity can often be expected when the high pressure is close by and the winds are light, whereas more cloud and the risk of showers may be expected during stronger winds and around weather fronts. The sunniest weather will always be towards the west coast and more generally across the north-western quarter of Scotland.

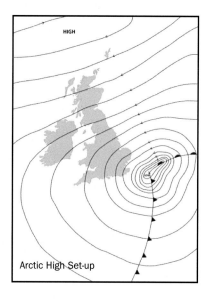

Arctic High Set-up

- Visibility is likely to be excellent outside of showers, especially during the cold winter months. Banks of hill fog are most likely on east-facing mountain slopes and in the east of the area.

- Most common during the winter to early spring months (December-March).

Atlantic High Set-up

■ High pressure ridges into the Atlantic Ocean west of the UK, either from the Azores High to the south or the Greenland High to the north, with low pressure centred over Scandinavia or continental Europe.

■ Typically results in an unsettled cool or cold northerly airflow across Scotland, with showers likely to be heaviest and most frequent in the north and east.

■ The West Highland area will tend to receive fewer showers and greater amounts of sunshine, with the sunniest weather towards the south-western quarter of the country. The frequency and intensity of showers is governed by proximity of the high pressure, wind strength and location of weather fronts.

■ Due to the cold Arctic origin of the air mass, air clarity and visibility are likely to be good or excellent at all times of the year, outside of passing showers.

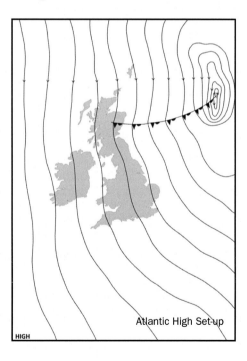

Atlantic High Set-up

HIGH

■ Banks of hill fog are most likely on north-facing mountain slopes, in the north and east of the area.

■ Most common during the winter to early spring months (December-March).

Atlantic Depression Set-up

■ The most common weather pattern with the frequent eastward movement of low pressure systems across Britain, the centre of the depressions tracking to the north of Scotland.

■ Produces the typically unsettled weather conditions, with the eastward movement of persistent bands of rain followed by showers, often accompanied by strong winds.

■ The West Highland area bears the brunt of the weather arriving from the Atlantic, resulting in the highest rainfall totals, strongest winds and extensive hill fog.

■ Common at any time of year but with the most severe depressions typically occurring in the autumn, when ex-hurricanes from central America are caught up in the jet stream and track eastward across the Atlantic to our shores.

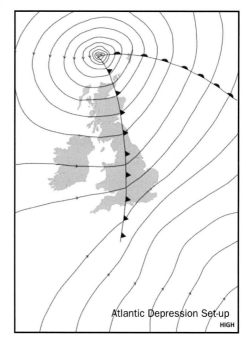

Atlantic Depression Set-up

HIGH

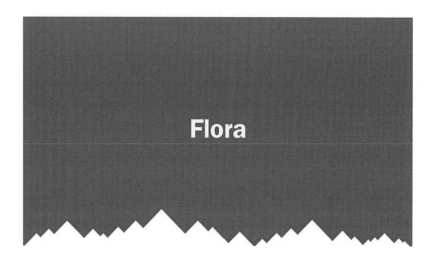

Flora

The flora of this area is adapted to the wild mountainous terrain and wet but relatively mild climate.

The greatest floral diversity is understandably in the glens, where most of the trees are found. These comprise a mixture of coniferous plantations (such as Leanachan Forest along the eastern margin of the Great Glen), deciduous forest, mainly comprising silver birch, rowan, willow, beech, alder and oak (such as along Glen Nevis), or mixed coniferous-deciduous forest. Due to increasing exposure at higher elevations, trees are very rare and sparse above the 450m contour. Low-growing plants in the glens include grass and heather, along with patches of bracken. Cotton grass is diagnostic of perennially wet and boggy areas, and walkers can use its presence to avoid such terrain.

At higher elevations, vegetation becomes increasingly patchy and dominated by low-growing and then ground-hugging species, adapted to high winds and freezing temperatures. Heather is common on some mountain slopes up to around the 900m contour, whereas other mountain slopes are mainly covered in grass or cotton grass up to these elevations. The bedrock geology plays an important role in determining floral species at lower altitudes.

Heather predominates on sandy well-drained soils weathered out of a granitic bedrock, such as the Carn Mor Dearg Massif, Coire Giubhsachan and Mullach nan Coirean, whereas grass is the main vegetation type on clayey less free-draining soils weathered out of a metamorphic bedrock, such as across much of the central-eastern Mamores and Aonach Beag Massif. The slope angle also plays a significant role, with gentler and therefore more stable slopes typically being far more vegetated than those which are steeper and more unstable. The latter are often covered in rocky outcrops and scree.

Above Munro level (914m), vegetation is much patchier and less diverse, mainly comprising tufts of grass and ground-hugging plants such as mosses and lichens. The stark difference in vegetation is a direct function of the transition from a temperate microclimate in the sheltered glens, to a harsh exposed Arctic climate on the highest summits of the Nevis Range (especially Ben Nevis and Aonach Beag). Large expanses of boulders or scree are often weathered out by fierce winds across the exposed Munro summits, although there are a few notable exceptions (such as the grassy summit ridge of Aonach Mor). The abundance and diversity of vegetation in this area is therefore strongly related to the degree of exposure.

Fauna

The diverse range of habitats across the Nevis and Mamore ranges results in an interesting array of faunal species, some of which are unique to the Scottish Highlands and rare or absent elsewhere in Great Britain or the world.

The forested glens, such as Glen Nevis or around Kinlochleven, are home to the pine marten, red squirrel, roe deer and rare wild cat. These animals are often shy and elusive, avoiding human contact and difficult to spot or photograph amongst the denser vegetation.

The pine marten (*Martes martes*) was once one of the most common carnivores across the British Isles, but extensive forest clearance and culling during the 1800s and early 1900s significantly reduced their numbers. Today the main British pine marten populations are located across the Highlands of Scotland, where historical pressures from human habitation have been less. Pine martens are largely nocturnal and rarely encountered by walkers, but can also be active during the day.

The red squirrel (*Sciurus vulgaris*) is native to Britain, however its populations in the UK have been put increasingly under threat following the introduction of grey squirrels from North America. Red squirrels have russet red fur and inhabit both coniferous and deciduous woodland, although the American grey squirrels appear to have a competitive advantage in the latter. Scotland reportedly holds about 75% of Britain's red squirrel population, and conservationist groups are working hard to stop the spread of grey squirrels northward across the country.

Roe deer (*Capreolus capreolus*) are native to the British Isles and can be found in lowland forest and grassland right across the UK. Deforestation and hunting resulted in roe deer becoming temporarily extinct across England by 1800, before being reintroduced with a resulting population recovery during the 19th and 20th centuries. These deer are smaller than many other deer species, weighing up to 25kg, with the males having correspondingly smaller antlers. They are however less common in the Fort William area than the much larger and more impressive red deer, due to the restricted distribution of their forested habitat.

The Scottish Wild Cat, Britain's only remaining wild cat, is critically endangered, with perhaps as few as 100 individuals or less remaining in the Scottish Highlands. Whilst efforts are being made to preserve the native wild populations, the future conservation status of this species in the wild is very uncertain.

At higher elevations, the bare mountainsides are home to the mountain hare and spectacular red deer, whose calls echo throughout the glens during the autumn rutting season.

The mountain hare (*Lepus timidus*) has inhabited Britain for at least the past 114,000 years, however indigenous populations have become confined to the Scottish Highlands. Reintroduced populations can also be found on the Isle of Man and in the Peak District. These mammals live only above the 500m contour in Scotland, where their coat changes from white or grey in winter (for camouflage against the winter snow) to a pale russet brown in summer.

The red deer (*Cervus elaphus*) is Britain's largest land mammal, with a reddish-brown to brown summer coat and a brown to grey winter coat. Red deer migrated across a land bridge from Europe into Britain about 11,000 years ago, before flooding of the North Sea and English Channel. These deer initially inhabited lowland forests nationwide across the country; however extensive forest clearances and hunting resulted in a confinement of populations towards the Scottish Highlands and south-west England during the 18th and 19th centuries, where they adapted to living on the bare exposed mountainsides. The impressive branched antlers are found on the males, which can weigh as much as 190kg.

High exposed rocky outcrops form the habitat for grouse and ptarmigan (*Lagopus* family), the grey rocks providing a suitable camouflage for these shy birds. Rare golden eagles also nest on such exposed rocky outcrops, far away from major walking routes and the possibility of discovery by mankind.

Red deer grazing the grassy western slopes of Ben Nevis

Thanks to the mild and humid summer climate, the vegetated glens play host to an abundance of insect species. Every walker in this area knows all too well about the prevalence of the Highland midge, mosquitoes and horseflies (described in the next dedicated section).

Several species of attractive and rare dragonflies are also found around boggy marshland at lower elevations. The white-faced darter (*Leuchorrhinia dubia*) is a small dragonfly which is found around peatbogs from the Midlands northwards. The males have a black abdomen with red and orange patches, whilst the females have a black abdomen marked with yellow patches. The northern emerald (*Somatochlora arctica*) is restricted to the western Highlands and parts of Ireland, with a bronze green thorax and a dark abdomen. The azure hawker (*Aeshna caerulea*) is only widespread across the Highlands of Scotland and has distinctive pale blue markings across the abdomen.

Several rare butterfly species also inhabit the glens and mountainsides of the area, including the chequered skipper, the mountain ringlet and the Scotch argus. The chequered skipper (*Carterocephalus palaemon*) was declared extinct in England in 1976 and is now only found across Lochaber, northern Argyll and Knoydart in Scotland. This butterfly is characterised by chequered yellow/brown markings on its wings and prefers sheltered south-facing slopes covered in purple moor-grass. The mountain ringlet (*Erebia epiphron*) is mainly found in Lochaber & Argyll (western Highlands), along with the Lake District in England, but only tends to emerge from the grass on bright sunny days. This attractive brown butterfly, typically found on mountain slopes between the 450m and 800m contours, may have been one of the first butterflies to return to the British Isles after the last ice age, as it prefers cool climates.

Midges, horseflies, mosquitoes and ticks

The mild and moist climate of the western Highlands provides the perfect breeding ground for a variety of insect species, some of which are scarce or absent elsewhere in Great Britain. These insects are mainly a problem during the warm summer months, typically May-September. They are also most prevalent in the sheltered vegetated glens, and rarely present much of a problem on higher slopes and mountain summits.

Midges

The Highland midge (*Culicoides impunctatus*) is undoubtedly the most annoying pest in the Scottish Highlands. The flies are very small but quickly become present in such vast numbers, getting into the eyes, ears and mouth, that the unfortunate walker has no option but to simply move somewhere else. Scottish midges are renowned for being much more vicious than other species in the family, the females mercilessly biting any piece of exposed skin they can find. Although the bites can be itchy, they tend to be small and fairly short-lived. The insects live in thick lush grass and progressively increase in numbers during the course of the summer months, peaking during July and August. During this time of year, midges plague the western half of Scotland along with parts of North-West England and Wales, but are scarce or absent across southern and eastern Britain, where the drier climate does not allow development of the thick lush grassy habitat in which this insect thrives. In general, midges are a minor irritation for walkers in the glens where there is an abundance of vegetation, whilst these insects cause negligible or no problems on higher more poorly vegetated slopes. Midges cause the most misery for campers or those trying to have a nice relaxing picnic in a scenic glen, for whom the following details should be noted:

- These tiny insects cannot fly in anything more than a light breeze, so they are scarce on windy days and windward slopes. Contrary to standard convention, it is often worthwhile seeking out a more exposed and breezy spot for a rest or picnic during summer in the western Highlands.

- Midges dislike strong hot sunshine and low humidity, so they are less of a nuisance during such rare summer days in the West Highland area. They also cannot fly through heavy rain.

- In general, midges take to the air in their greatest numbers during mild evenings when the wind falls. However these flies can be tenacious throughout the day during humid weather, such as when the wind drops after a passing rain shower, when they often emerge from the lush wet vegetation in their droves.

- The best advice, should midges start to cause an irritation, is simply to keep moving. On humid days with light winds, it may not be possible to stop for a relaxing picnic – you may have to eat on the go. Killing the little creatures as they land on your body or in the air is generally futile, as they are so numerous.

■ Leaving less skin exposed to the air reduces the surface area that midges can bite and therefore reduces the irritation.

■ A number of midge repellent products have been developed in recent years to try and make the human body smell less attractive to these insects. These can be purchased from many shops in Fort William or from some campsites. Some are more effective than others. Whilst many products reduce the number that start biting, the flies still seem attracted to the human body and swarm irritatingly around.

■ "Midgeater" machines have been introduced to many of the larger and more established campsites in the West Highlands during the 21st Century. These machines attract the insects by releasing CO_2 gas, which the female midge mistakes for the emissions of a living organism, whereupon they are sucked into a collecting bag and cannot escape. Whilst a small number of these machines no doubt reduce the problem, it would probably take a large number to be an effective solution.

Horseflies and mosquitoes

Horseflies and mosquitoes, like midges, are mainly encountered in the glens and are less of a problem for the mountain walker at higher and more exposed altitudes.

Horseflies, the common name given to members of the insect family *Tabanidae*, are significantly larger than the tiny midge and present in much smaller numbers, but the females of the species inflict a much nastier bite. These flies can be found throughout much of the British Isles during summer and are especially prevalent near to animals such as horses, hence their name. A sharp pin-prick is often felt when these flies break the skin, and these bites often become large and irritatingly itchy. Instant swatting is often the best way to kill the insects, which tend to react very quickly and are often difficult to catch otherwise. Horseflies can often be distinguished from other flying insects by their larger size and cunning attitude, always trying to find the ideal point to land on their victim when they least suspect it. Trying to shake the fly off while it's biting is often ineffective - if they get any hint that you are about to swat them, they will take to the air, only to return to another part of the body a few seconds later.

Mosquitoes, members of the family *Culicidae*, are not only found in the West Highlands but right across the British Isles and elsewhere in the world in close proximity to animals or livestock. Mosquitoes are perhaps best known for being a common transmitter of malaria in equatorial regions. Fortunately this is not a problem in Britain, although they can still carry other diseases. These flies are again significantly larger than midges and present in much fewer numbers, but can be distinguished from horseflies by their larger wings and legs, similar to those of a crane fly. Mosquitoes can also inflict a nasty bite but tend to be less cunning, less persistent and easier to swat than horseflies. Unlike horseflies, a mosquito bite is often not felt at the time and only becomes apparent later on, when an itchy lump develops.

The following points of information and advice should be noted regarding horseflies and mosquitoes:

■ In contrast to midges, horseflies are most prevalent on hot sunny summer days, when sometimes two or three can appear at once and tenaciously attempt to feed. Walkers should therefore always be on the lookout for these flies under such conditions, although they can be a nuisance at any time during the summer months.

■ Keeping as much skin covered as possible can help to reduce the surface area that these flies target. However this is often ineffective for horseflies, which can bite through several layers of clothing.

■ The application of antihistamine cream can help to reduce the itchiness of the nasty bites inflicted by these insects. However if the bite starts to significantly swell over the following few hours or days, then medical advice should be sought as there may be a risk of infection.

Ticks

Ticks are members of the spider family (arachnids) and are distributed nationwide across the British Isles, anywhere in close proximity to wild animals or livestock. These initially small spider-like creatures feed on blood from whichever living organism they can get onto, progressively swelling up until eventually they naturally detach and drop to the ground again. Once they have digested all of this blood, they are ready for the next victim. Ticks are mainly a problem where there is thick and tall vegetation, especially bracken which reaches above boot length in height. Ticks in the bracken can then detach as your leg swipes through, before crawling over your body to find an ideal point to penetrate the skin and start feeding. As ticks feed from a variety of different animals, in the West Highlands most likely deer or sheep, they are excellent transmitters of disease. The most common disease in Britain is Lyme disease, a potentially serious condition; cases have started to increase in recent years.

The following preventative and recovery advice is suggested for ticks:

■ Avoid brushing through areas of thick or dense vegetation above boot height, especially bracken. Should ticks be present in this vegetation, it is very easy for them to detach onto trousers or legs.

■ It is worthwhile spending a few minutes checking your clothes for the small spider-like creatures after a day out in the hills. If located, then these ticks can be removed before they have chance to penetrate the skin.

■ It is advisable to wear long trousers that completely cover the skin if it is necessary to walk through dense vegetation, so that any ticks will detach onto the trousers and not directly onto your skin. These trousers can then be inspected at the end of the day, whereas without trousers the unnoticed tick may break the skin before the end of the walk.

■ The first sign that you have a tick will be a persistently itchy bite, which upon inspection will reveal the small black arachnid at the centre. Various methods are advocated for their removal, including drowning them in water and soaking them with alcohol, which forces them to release naturally. The best method however is probably to carefully and slowly remove the tick with a pair of tweezers. Whichever method is used, the most important points are to remove the tick as soon as it is noticed, and to make sure that its head and all mouthparts are removed from the bite to reduce the risk of infection. The bite may remain itchy for the next day or two, however a marked swelling or development of a characteristic red ring around the bite are likely to be symptoms of Lyme disease. Medical advice should be sought as soon as such symptoms are noticed, as Lyme disease is easily treatable with antibiotics if caught early, but can be disabling if allowed to develop.

Essential equipment and advice for the mountains

Some basic equipment, supplies and knowledge are essential to safely enjoy walks in the mountains, with these essentials differing somewhat between summer and winter conditions. Summer conditions are defined here as the few months of the year when snow and ice recede from the highest peaks, with no specialist equipment (i.e. ropes, crampons, hard hats, ice axes etc.) required. Summer conditions normally occur from late June or July until September in the area, with a bit of variation from year to year. It is important to note that winter snow and ice may not clear from the higher summits of the Nevis Range, especially the summit plateau of Ben Nevis, until well into July during cold summers.

For summer conditions, the well-equipped walker will carry or wear the following:

- **A knowledge of the latest mountain weather forecast from the Met Office.** This should be routinely checked at the start of the day, to decide if the planned route is suitable for the predicted weather conditions. Many of the ridge routes become dangerous undertakings during strong winds and there is a risk of navigational difficulties on many higher level routes during

48

persistent dense hill fog, including on the summit plateau of Ben Nevis.

- **Strong, grippy and ideally waterproof walking boots.** These are essential for all of the routes described in this book, which involve walking over rough or rocky terrain at some stage. Trainers are made for exercise on an even regular surface and do not give the same level of grip across wild mountainous terrain. They are also likely to be easily destroyed when traversing scree slopes, especially those composed of sharp angular quartzite blocks. This advice is evidenced by the fact that many walkers who bail out of the Mountain Track ascent up Ben Nevis are wearing very inappropriate footwear, even high heels, sandals or flip-flops.

- **A strong lightweight rucksack, with sufficient capacity to carry all of the required equipment for the day.** It is ideal if the rucksack has a waterproof covering in the event of wet weather, especially if valuable items such as mobile phones are to be kept inside.

- **Several layers of clothing, ideally thin layers that wick away sweat from the body.** These could include several T-shirts or thin sleeved jumpers and can be bought from all major outdoor shops across the country. The number of layers depends on the temperature and wind chill, but it is often a good idea to carry several extra additional layers in the rucksack in case of unexpected weather. There are several advantages to "layering" as opposed to wearing one or two thick bulky garments:

  - It is inevitable that the body temperature will rise and any walker will sweat during the physical exertion involved with a steep mountain ascent. These thin layers can therefore be removed easily as required during the climb, then replaced if cold weather is encountered near the mountain summit.

  - Wearing clothes made from a fabric that wicks away sweat

keeps the body much drier, not only adding comfort during the climb but keeping the walker warmer during cold or windy weather. These layers are normally made from polyester or sometimes wool and are especially important for the "base layer", the first layer of clothing in contact with your skin.

Wearing several layers provides extra insulation for the body and retains a greater amount of heat, due to air trapped between the layers. This is analogous to the application of bubble wrap to insulate a greenhouse, where the air trapped within each bubble provides the insulation. Wearing three or four thin layers can be more effective than wearing one thick fleecy coat and allows greater flexibility during movement.

■ **Warm, waterproof but lightweight coat, hat, trousers and gloves.** Even if the weather is forecast to be predominantly warm and sunny, unpredictable weather changes can occur. Any frequent walker in the hills is likely to be caught out by unpredicted weather at some point during their time in the Highlands. Warm clothing can always stay in the rucksack if the weather is warm, and it's always better to be safe than sorry. In particular, weather conditions in the glens often have little bearing on temperatures and wind speeds on the high exposed summits and should never be used as a guide to what to expect. The coat should not be too heavy and bulky, as such garments reduce flexibility when walking and consequently more energy is consumed while moving.

■ **Clean fresh water.** This can be collected from suitable rivers on the route; however it is advisable to bring some at the start of the day. For the longer routes in this book, where water is only available at the start and end of a long day, it may be necessary to fill up two water bottles before ascending to higher elevations. More water will always be required when hill walking in hot, sunny, or humid weather. Water inherently adds extra weight in the rucksack, consuming more energy during the climb, so it is important to find the correct balance and you should carry no more water than you expect to need.

- **Energy foods.** During major climbs it is better to eat in a "little but often" manner, by having a number of short snack breaks rather than one big lunch stop. Foods rich in carbohydrates are the most important to provide quick energy boosts. These could include bananas, chocolate or snack bars in addition to sandwiches. Some food with a higher salt content is also important to replace that lost by sweating and prevent hyponatraemia, an illness developed when sodium ion content in the blood falls below a certain threshold and cells can no longer absorb water. Large meals at the beginning and end of the day are also beneficial, to fuel the body before the start of the walk and then replace calories burned afterwards. At least one hour should be set aside after an early morning meal before starting a long mountain climb.

- **Communication devices such as a mobile phone, satellite phone or two-way radio.** Mobile phone coverage tends to be very limited in the glens; you may get a signal on higher slopes and mountain summits, although it should never be relied upon. A satellite phone should work wherever the phone has a clear pathway to an overhead satellite. Two-way radio will only work effectively where each radio has a direct line of communication with the other, without any mountains in the way. It is good practice to leave an outline of the planned walking route, including an expected return time, with your accommodation so that an alarm can be raised if necessary. In the unlikely event of an accident, dial 999 and ask for mountain rescue. The Lochaber Mountain Rescue Team assists with accidents in this area. It was established in the 1960s and has a team of around 40 unpaid volunteers.

- **A detailed topographic map at 1:25,000 scale.** The sketch maps accompanying each walking route in this book are intended as a guide and are insufficient for use in the hills. The best modern topographic maps for this area are:

  - Harvey Superwalker Map, Ben Nevis. This map is usefully waterproof and also contains a 1:12,500 scale enlargement across the summit plateau of Ben Nevis.

  - Ordnance Survey Explorer Map 1:25,000 Ben Nevis & Fort William (Sheet 392).

- **A compass and the knowledge of how to use it (with an accompanying topographic map)**, in case dense fog creates navigational difficulties.

- **A basic first-aid kit** to treat minor injuries on the mountainside.

- **Sun cream.** This is essential in summer, as it is much easier to burn when mountain walking at higher altitudes, even on a fairly cloudy day. It is also easy to get sunburn when there is still extensive snow cover on the ground in early spring. The high albedo of the white snow pack effectively reflects the sun's rays back on the walker, significantly amplifying its effect.

- On the longer routes of "Very Hard" grade, a **torch and some sort of basic emergency shelter** may be advisable pieces of kit in case the walk takes longer than anticipated and darkness falls.

Winter conditions, defined here as when snow and ice cover the summits, require a new set of skills, experience and important additional and rather more specialist equipment. It is often underestimated how much more energy is consumed when walking or climbing across snow or ice, and when combined with the shorter length of the winter day, normally only shorter walks are possible. The following **additional** equipment is required for winter conditions:

- **Good quality crampons.** These normally strap onto the base of your walking boots, comprising a series of metal spikes which provide excellent grip when ascending slopes of firm frozen snow or ice. They are less effective in deep fresh snow, when walking any distance in any footwear is extremely energy-consuming.

- **An ice axe** for extra stability, safety and reassurance on steep snow slopes or narrow ridges.

- **A greater emphasis on warm clothing, including a thick coat, warm fleecy hat and gloves.**

- **Sun glasses or goggles**, to reduce glare off the snow pack and decrease the risk of snow blindness and disorientation.

To preserve this spectacular mountainous environment for future generations to enjoy, adhere to the following rules when out in the hills:

- Always take non-biodegradable litter home with you. Not only does the presence of litter tarnish this beautiful landscape, it poses a health hazard for the local wildlife that live here. Most mountain walkers abide by this rule without thinking twice, but there is still a small but noticeable minority who don't. Litter is a particular problem along the Mountain Track and at the summit of Ben Nevis due to the vast number of walkers.

- If disposing of food waste that will biodegrade naturally (such as a banana skin or orange peel), only do so in small quantities and bury it out of sight so that no other walker would know of its presence.

- Always stick to the main paths as much as possible. Walking off the path widens it and causes noticeable erosion, increasing its visual effect on the landscape. Footpath erosion is again unfortunately all too visible on the Mountain Track up Ben Nevis and this track is visible from some distance away as a result.

- Do not take large pieces of rock away from the mountains with you. Not only will they feel like a lead weight in your rucksack, but if everyone did it then eventually there would be nothing of the mountains left.

- The simple but commonly used motto is: **take nothing but photographs and leave nothing but footprints**.

Drinking water in the mountains

Drinking plenty of fluids to replace those lost through sweat and exertion is essential when walking in the mountains. The amount of fluid required increases when climbing in the warmer temperatures of summer. It is often impractical to carry all the fluids required for a long day in the hills from the start, and more convenient to regularly fill up with water from streams during the walk. This of course can carry inherent health risks through water-borne bacteria, which may breed within water of a suitable temperature or be introduced by a decaying animal carcass which interacts with a neighbouring water source (most likely sheep or deer). However these risks are low if the following advice is followed:

■ Always fill up bottles from water that is fast-flowing and icy cold in temperature. Never fill up from still (and potentially stagnant) water bodies such as lochs or other pools, or anywhere downstream from such water bodies. A good topographic map is useful for this. The still water in lochs will warm up during the day, with infrequent replenishment and recycling of the water, increasing the risk of bacterial contamination over time.

■ Ideally always fill up from a stream as close as possible to its source, where it emerges as a spring from the mountainside. The further the water travels across the surface, the higher the risk of contamination.

■ Avoid filling up from major river systems such as the River Nevis or River Leven. These rivers have drained a large catchment area, with an increased risk of contamination.

■ Only fill up with water that is crystal clear and has no discolouration of any kind. A brown discolouration often occurs where a stream has drained through peaty or boggy terrain, whilst a green discolouration may be due to the presence of algae.

■ Once collected, do not allow the water in your flask to warm up during the day. Any water that is no longer ice cold in temperature should be emptied and replaced.

■ Streams which are likely to contain suitable water for drinking are highlighted on each walk; however circumstances change and these water sources should still be checked against the above criteria. The key point is, if in doubt for any reason, do not drink.

Tips for mountain photography

The dramatic mountainous landscape in this area lends itself to the amateur photographer, with the opportunity to obtain some really stunning shots. The type and model of camera used will of course play a significant role, but with the hints and tips below, it should be possible to capture some truly stunning mountain photographs with any type of digital camera, avoiding the amateur photographer's curse of dull and uninteresting "flat light".

■ The most stunning vistas occur when meteorological conditions favour extreme air clarity and therefore excellent visibility. The greatest air clarity tends to occur in winter or spring, when northerly or easterly winds bring in a cold clear air mass from the Arctic or continental Europe. Reasonable air clarity can also occur under similar cool conditions in summer; however a haze often develops at warmer times of the year, masking distant mountains. Many of the wintry photographs in this book were taken during a cold easterly or north-easterly high-pressure dominated set-up during late winter and early spring.

■ Mountain photographers often avoid taking photographs in the middle of sunny days, especially during summer. The high light intensity will tend to bleach the photograph, whilst the high-angled sun will fail to highlight any interesting features of the mountain. Instead aim to take photographs during the early morning or late afternoon/evening when the sun is at a low angle, casting shadows across the landscape and picking out impressive rock features and structures that may not have been apparent under the midday sun. A setting or rising sun can also bathe the mountain scenery in attractive reds, oranges or yellows, making the landscape really come to life. However always leave adequate time to descend off the mountainside before darkness falls.

■ Aim to shoot photos with the low-angled sun to one side of your subject. Taking photos towards the sun will result in bleaching, whilst shadows will be obscured and the landscape appear flatter and less interesting when taking photos with the sun directly behind you.

■ On bright sunny days, including a section of clear blue sky or fluffy cumulus clouds will add extra vivid colours and contrast to the photo.

■ On dull or cloudy days, taking in too much grey and boring sky will often have a negative effect and detract attention from the landscape. Under cloudy conditions, aim to focus only on the mountain or landscape, taking in as little sky as possible.

■ Including an interesting rock feature or structure in the foreground of the photo, backed by a dramatic landscape, can help to add scale and dimension to a mountain photo.

■ A covering of winter snow will often add a very different feel and character to a mountain or landscape, as the photos in this book aim to illustrate. Under calm conditions, a thick blanket of snow can fall and cover a mountain fairly evenly. However this snow is often redistributed to collect in sheltered corries, crevasses and river valleys, highlighting these features against the otherwise bare mountainside and more exposed features such as ridges and arêtes, where the snow and ice cover can be thinned or stripped off by fierce winds.

■ Patience is a virtue when it comes to mountain photography. Waiting until that perfect moment when a ray of sunlight breaks through the clouds to highlight the mountain of interest, whilst the surroundings are cast in shadow, can really emphasise the centrepiece of your photograph.

■ The different seasons bring out an interesting variety of colours in the western Highlands. The mild and moist summer months encourage vivid greens as the mountainsides become bathed in lush vegetation. Heather-covered mountain slopes can become tinged with pink as this low-growing shrub comes into flower. Autumn is the season of oranges and russet browns, as the colour changes on the bracken and grass in response to the cooling temperatures and shorter days. Meanwhile towards the second half of autumn, the first snow falls and splatters the higher peaks, creating a pleasant contrast. Winter and early spring are characterised by the white of the snow-covered mountainsides and the dark grey or brown colour of the dormant vegetation. You can create an interesting series of images by photographing the same mountain from the same location at different times during the year, to illustrate how the colour (and therefore atmosphere and mood) of the scene changes with the seasons.

Transport and accommodation

There is no doubt that a car is the easiest and most flexible method of transport around the Fort William area. However some of the routes in this book start and end at different locations, and in these instances, using public transport can be advantageous. There is a limited Stagecoach bus service (41, 42) from Fort William town centre as far as the Lower Falls Waterfall in Glen Nevis during the summer, located just over 2km down the valley from the car park at the road end. There are more regular Scottish Citylink and Stagecoach (19, 41) buses from Fort William town centre northward to Torlundy, the Nevis Range Ski Centre and on to Spean Bridge, as well as southward to Kinlochleven and Glencoe (Stagecoach 44). Up-to-date timetables should be referred to for precise times.

For those without a car, Fort William itself is fairly easy to get to, with Scottish Citylink, Stagecoach and Shiel Buses collectively linking Fort William with Glasgow, Inverness, Oban, Edinburgh, Mallaig, the Isle of Skye and many places in between. Fort William is also located on the West Highland Railway Line, allowing easy connection to the major cities in Scotland and across the UK. Air travel to the area is rather more problematic, with the closest international airports located a few hours' drive away at Inverness or Glasgow.

Fort William or lower Glen Nevis represent the best bases for exploring the Nevis Range and western Mamores, from the Ring of Steall mountains westward. Walkers are spoilt for choice in Fort William, with accommodation to suit most budgets including a whole host of B&Bs, hotels, campsites, guest houses and self-catering chalets. In lower Glen Nevis, there is a large campsite, youth hostel and further B&Bs.

Kinlochleven represents a closer base from which to explore the eastern Mamores. Although somewhat more isolated from the main A82, located 10 miles down a winding and undulating road along which some locals attempt to do motorway speeds, Kinlochleven and its environs also offer a decent array of accommodation including hotels, guest houses, B&Bs, hostels and campsites.

THE PEAKS

Ben Nevis

Munro Number: **1**

Nevis Range Number: **1**

Height: **1,344m (4,409ft)**

Associated Tops: **Carn Dearg (NW Top, 1221m, 4006ft), Carn Dearg (SW Top, 1020m, 3346ft), Meall an t-Suidhe (711m, 2333ft)**

Translation: **Evil, venomous or cloud mountain**

Ben Nevis from Carn Mor Dearg

Aonach Beag

Munro Number: **7**

Nevis Range Number: **2**

Height: **1,234m (4,049ft)**

Associated Tops: **Stob Coire Bhealaich (1101m, 3612ft), Sgurr a' Bhuic (963m, 3159ft)**

Translation: **Little Ridge**

Pronunciation: **Oonach Beg, with the "ch" pronounced like that in "loch"**

The Aonach Beag Massif from Glen Nevis

Aonach Mor

Munro Number: **8**

Nevis Range Number: **3**

Height: **1,221m (4,006ft)**

Associated Tops: **Stob an Cul Choire (1068m, 3504ft)**

Translation: **Big Ridge**

Pronunciation: **Oonach Morr**

Aonach Mor from Roy Bridge, Glen Spean

Carn Mor Dearg

Munro Number: **9**

Nevis Range Number: **4**

Height: **1,220m (4,003ft)**

Associated Tops: **Carn Dearg Meadhonach (1179m, 3868ft), Carn Beag Dearg (1010m, 3314ft)**

Translation: **Big Red Cairn**

Pronunciation: **Carn Morr Jerrg**

Carn Mor Dearg from Carn Dearg Meadhonach

Binnein Mor

Munro Number: **28**

Mamore Range Number: **1**

Height: **1,130m (3,707ft)**

Associated Tops: **Unnamed South Top (1062m, 3484ft), Sgurr Eilde Beag (956m, 3136ft)**

Translation: **Big Peak**

Pronunciation: **Beenyen Morr**

Binnein Mor from Sgurr Eilde Beag

Sgurr a' Mhaim

Munro Number: **51**

Mamore Range Number: **2**

Height: **1,099m (3,606ft)**

Associated Tops: **Sgurr an Iubhair (1001m, 3284ft), Stob Coire a' Mhail (980m, 3215ft)**

Translation: **Peak of the Breast**

Pronunciation: **Sgurr a' Vaim**

Sgurr a' Mhaim from Glen Nevis, as a herd of red deer assemble in the foreground

Na Gruagaichean

Munro Number: **74**

Mamore Range Number: **3**

Height: **1,056m (3,465ft)**

Associated Tops: **Unnamed NW Top (1041m, 3415ft)**

Translation: **The Maidens**

Pronunciation: **Na Gruageechan, with the "ch" pronounced like that in "loch"**

Na Gruagaichean from Binnein Mor's South Top

Am Bodach

Munro Number: **99**

Mamore Range Number: **4**

Height: **1,032m (3,386ft)**

Associated Tops: **Sgurr an Iubhair (1001m, 3284ft)**

Translation: **The Old Man**

Pronunciation: **Am Boddach**

Am Bodach from Stob Coire a' Chairn

Sgurr Eilde Mor

Munro Number: **123**

Mamore Range Number: **5**

Height: **1,010m (3,314ft)**

Associated Tops: **-**

Translation: **The Big Peak of the Hind**

Pronunciation: **Sgurr Aider Morr**

Sgurr Eilde Mor and frozen Lochan Coire an Lochain from Sgurr Eilde Beag

71

Stob Ban

Munro Number: **138**

Mamore Range Number: **6**

Height: **999m (3,278ft)**

Associated Tops: -

Translation: **Fair or White Peak**

Pronunciation: **Stob Baan**

Stob Ban and Lochan Coire nam Miseach from the western
slopes of Sgurr an Iubhair

An Gearanach

Munro Number: **167**

Mamore Range Number: **7**

Height: **982m (3,222ft)**

Associated Tops: **An Garbhanach (975m, 3199ft)**

Translation: **The Complainer**

Pronunciation: **An Gerranach**

An Gearanach and An Garbhanach from the cairn on Stob Coire a' Chairn

Stob Coire a' Chairn

Munro Number: **168**

Mamore Range Number: **8**

Height: **981m (3,218ft)**

Associated Tops: -

Translation: **Peak of the Corrie of the Cairn**

Pronunciation: **Stob Coire a' Harn**

Stob Coire a' Chairn and Coire a' Chairn from the northern slopes of Meall an Doire Dharaich

Binnein Beag

Munro Number: **230**

Mamore Range Number: **9**

Height: **943m (3,094ft)**

Associated Tops: **-**

Translation: **Small Peak**

Pronunciation: **Beenyen Beg**

Binnein Beag from Binnein Mor's north ridge

Mullach nan Coirean

Munro Number: **234**

Mamore Range Number: **10**

Height: **939m (3,081ft)**

Associated Tops: **Unnamed SE Top (917m, 3008ft), Meall a' Chaorainn (910m, 2986ft)**

Translation: **Hill of the Corries**

Pronunciation: **Mullach nan Coyan**

Mullach nan Coirean from the road end in Glen Nevis

Introduction to the routes

Grading

The following walks are graded from very easy through to very hard, to give the reader some idea of the difficulty level for each route. The grading level used here assumes some prior degree of Munro climbing experience in Scotland, though none of the routes require the use of any specialist equipment (i.e. ropes) during fine summer conditions. However, good strong waterproof footwear is essential for all of the routes described here, including the 'very easy' grade, which often still involve sections of rough or rocky terrain.

The grading here applies to summer conditions only, when winter snow and ice recede from the higher peaks, which may not occur on the higher summits of the Nevis Range until July. Many walks from medium grade upward become serious undertakings under the snow and ice of winter, and should only be attempted by experienced mountaineers with specialist equipment for winter walking (i.e. an ice axe and crampons), and even for them some steep or exposed sections may become dangerous and impassable. These graded routes should provide multiple options for any explorer in the area, from the valley wanderer to the super fit multi-Munro bagger.

■ **Very easy grade.** Walks graded at this level involve a total ascent of up to a few hundred metres and are fairly short, able to be completed in a few hours or less. These routes are ideal for those who want to explore the area but do not have the fitness, stamina or desire to climb any of the high mountain peaks. These walks typically follow low level trails through the glens, wind around the mountains or climb some of the lower hills, but more than the other routes described here, they tend to be plagued by midges during favourable weather conditions in high summer.

■ **Easy grade.** A reasonable level of fitness is necessary for routes of this grade and higher, as climbing starts to become a more important element of the walk. Walks graded as easy provide a greater opportunity to explore the area, venturing away from the more popular walking trails through the glens and ascending into this beautiful wild and rugged landscape, though not reaching Munro level. These walks can be regarded as ideal "warm up" routes for higher Munro expeditions in coming days, or are useful alternatives when the higher Munro summits are shrouded in hill fog.

■ **Medium grade.** Walks of this grade start to tackle and link some of the easier Munro summits in the area, with increasing levels of fitness and stamina required. These walks involve some steep ascents and descents and include some short sections of optional scrambling (i.e. use of the hands as well as the feet for extra stability), which can largely be circumvented on small paths. Walks of this grade and higher become much more serious expeditions under the snow and ice of winter, when crampons, an ice axe and prior experience under such conditions are required.

■ **Hard grade.** Walks of this grade and higher are more serious mountain expeditions under summer conditions, linking some of the higher summits in the area and requiring a high level of fitness and stamina. These walks often involve sections of exposed but fairly easy scrambling, requiring a good sense of balance and a head for heights, along with some steep descents and ascents on slippery scree. These routes are inadvisable during high winds and in the middle of winter due to the short length of the day. Only highly experienced winter walkers with the proper equipment should attempt these routes when under snow/ice.

■ **Very hard grade.** The highest grade, these walks are reserved for the super fit and experienced mountain walker or scrambler with very high levels of fitness and stamina. These routes link a number of the high Munro summits via exciting ridges, involving sections of fairly easy but exposed scrambling with multiple steep descents and re-ascents often on slippery scree. These routes are inadvisable under winter conditions due to their distance, difficulty and shorter length of the day.

Layout

Each walking route is accompanied by a simplified sketch map highlighting the route. These maps are intended as a guide only and should always be used in conjunction with a detailed topographic map when out in the mountains. The topographic features in the walking area are named in Scottish Gaelic; therefore a basic dictionary is included on the next page to understand the English meaning of these features.

Walking profiles are also displayed for each route, highlighting:

■ The location of the main and steepest ascents and descents on the route.

■ The generalised vegetation and terrain encountered, along with the location of narrow or exposed ridges.

■ The quality of the path and location of any sections of scrambling.

■ Nature of the solid bedrock throughout the walk, normally corresponding to the rock outcropping at the surface, except for in the glens where this may be covered by superficial sediments such as Quaternary alluvium or glaciogenic deposits (known to geologists as "drift").

■ The location of potentially suitable springs and streams to fill up water bottles.

Gaelic	English translation
Beag	Small, little
Meadhonach	Medium
Mor	Big
Dearg	Red
Ban	White, pale
Dubh	Dark
Allt	River, burn, stream
Coire	Corrie
Aonach	Ridge
Binnein, Stob, Sgurr	Peak
Ben	Mountain
Meall	Hill
Mhuilinn	Mill
Carn	Cairn

Basic Scottish Gaelic-English dictionary for the topographic
features of the walking area

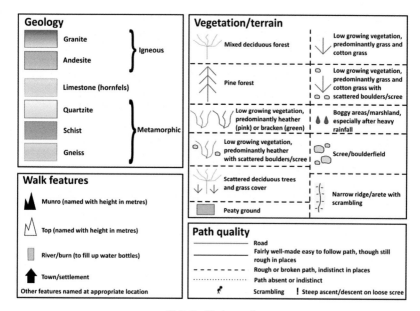

Walk Profile Legend

Please note the changing scales on these walking profiles, due to significant variations in length of the graded walks. A generic legend for all of the profiles is provided above.

Route 1:

Steall Waterfall and the Steall Ruins

This fine, gentle walk can be taken at an easy pace, allowing the walker to explore beautiful Glen Nevis and stare in awe up at the neighbouring high summits of the southern Nevis Range and Mamores to either side. This route is ideal for new explorers to the area, or for those who do not have the desire (or fitness and stamina) to climb the high mountain peaks, with an option to continue as far up into increasingly remote Glen Nevis as desired.

The contrasting tight confines of the narrow Nevis Gorge, often described as Himalayan in character, followed by the open Steall Meadows and magnificent white slash of the Steall Waterfall, are a must see for any walker in the Scottish Highlands. This route is often very popular with families and Munro-baggers alike during fine weather throughout much of the year, although many casual walkers do not make it much further than the Steall Meadows or Steall Waterfall. Glen Nevis offers many fine opportunities for a scenic picnic, however unfortunately can be plagued by midges, horseflies and mosquitoes during favourable weather conditions in high summer.

Steall Waterfall and the Steall Ruins	
Difficulty	Very Easy
Distance	3.8 km (2.4 miles) return to base of Steall Waterfall, 5 km (3.2 miles) return to Steall Ruins
Cumulative ascent	90m to base of Steall Waterfall/Steall Ruins
Approximate time taken	1 hour return to Steall Waterfall, 1.5 hours return to Steall Waterfall and Steall Ruins
Munros	-
Subsidiary Tops	-
Advisories	• Strong, grippy and waterproof footwear essential • Rough and rocky path through the Nevis Gorge • Boggy sections in the Steall Meadows • Slippery rocks beneath the Steall Waterfall • Midges, horse flies and mosquitoes can be bad in summer

Route 1 Summary

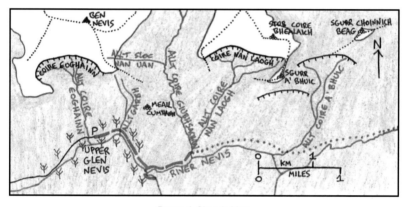

Route 1 Sketch Map

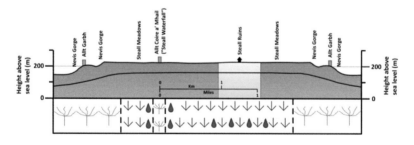

Route 1 Walk Profile

83

Take the initially well-made path heading eastward from the far end of the popular car park at the road end in Glen Nevis. The path soon turns towards the ENE and starts to ascend through deciduous forest of predominantly silver birch, rowan and willow, before becoming increasingly rough and rocky, as it clings firstly to the steep southern slopes of Ben Nevis and then the steep western slopes of Meall Cumhann. The path crosses numerous streams draining these steep slopes and contours high above the River Nevis, which crashes over immense blocks of schist the size of small houses in a series of foaming and roaring waterfalls and torrents. The Steall Waterfall makes fleeting appearances through the forest during the early part of the walk, a magnificent white slash of foaming water plunging more than 100m down a rugged wall of solid schist.

A close examination of the schist at the eastern end of the Nevis Gorge reveals the presence of many tight parasitic folds and distinctive veins of pure white quartz, both formed as a result of the immense temperatures and pressures involved with metamorphism of the Dalradian sedimentary rocks during the Grampian Orogeny (480-460 million years ago).

The tight confines of the gorge suddenly open out into the spacious Steall Meadows, with the steep partially-forested and grassy slopes of An Gearanach rising up at the far south-eastern end, high above the great white slash of the Steall Waterfall. Steall Meadows used to be a large flat-bottomed loch, until the waters finally broke through a solid rock backstop at the western end. The loch then subsequently drained through the Nevis Gorge, leaving this grassy, boggy and peaceful meadow, home to countless midges, horseflies and mosquitoes. The vast wooded northern slopes of Sgurr a' Mhaim form the abrupt southern wall of the valley, with the quartzite summit out of sight from the valley floor.

Continue on the path across a sub-horizontal gradient directly towards the Steall Waterfall and An Gearanach. Shortly before the main path curves round to the east and climbs over some blocks of schist, a well-made path branches off to the right (south), heading towards a peculiar wire bridge across the River Nevis. This is the primary means of crossing the river, however when the water level is low, it may be possible to cross just upstream from the bridge using a serious of rocks as stepping stones, or wading through in bare feet. The crossing of the bridge involves two wire rails at the top for hand holds and a solid thicker wire at the base to inch your feet along, and is best taken relatively slowly as the wires tend to wobble and sway somewhat through the middle section. At the far end there's a climb onto a solid boulder of schist, below which the deepest part of the River Nevis flows adjacent to the bank.

Once the river has been crossed, continue SE past the Steall Hut (private and owned by the Lochaber Mountaineering Club) on a path to reach the Allt Coire a' Mhail, the river that forms the Steall Waterfall immediately above. Below the crashing and foaming waters of the Steall Waterfall are numerous angular blocks of slippery wet schist, around which the water tumbles and cascades. The Steall Waterfall, when viewed from beneath, is very impressive and loud. Foaming water crashes down numerous terraces of solid schist, sending off a fine misty spray which wets everything in the vicinity. The waterfall is particularly impressive if the Allt Coire a' Mhail is in spate after heavy rainfall, when a roaring torrent rages over these terraces as the water makes its tumultuous journey towards the River Nevis.

Return via the same route, back across the wire bridge to reach the main path through Glen Nevis. To continue to Steall Ruins, turn right (east) on the main path through Glen Nevis and clamber easily round some blocks of schist adjacent to the River Nevis, to reach a large shingle beach. This can be partially or completely flooded when the river is in spate, but otherwise it is a fine place to bathe on a hot day, with a fine view of the awe-inspiring Steall Waterfall. Locate a dirt path running along the northern bank of the river, just upstream from the shingle beach, and follow this to reach a wooden bridge across the Allt Coire Giubhsachan, a major tributary to the River Nevis. This river has drained from Coire Giubhsachan, a beautiful corrie situated in a spectacular location between the high summits of Aonach Beag, Carn Mor Dearg and the CMD Arête (**Route 6**). Cross this bridge to reach the Steall Ruins on the opposite side, perched beneath the steep southern slopes of Aonach Beag and Sgurr a' Bhuic. The Steall Ruins comprise the remains of two houses built in the late 1700s and occupied by shepherds until the 1940s, after which they became deserted and the neglected stone buildings were weathered by the elements to their current ruined state.

From here it is possible to continue along a rough path up into the increasingly remote upper portion of Glen Nevis, as far as time, weather or energy permit. To return, trace the outbound route back through the Steall Meadows and Nevis Gorge, to reach the car park at the road end.

Mullach nan Coirean and Sgurr a' Mhaim from the Nevis Gorge

The Steall Waterfall & An Gearanach from the entrance to
Steall Meadows in mid-summer

The Steall Waterfall & An Gearanach from the entrance to Steall Meadows in winter

Ben Nevis and the entrance to Nevis Gorge from Steall Meadows

The author crossing the wire bridge across the River Nevis

The frozen Steall Waterfall

Icicles along the bank of the River Nevis, with the frozen Steall Waterfall behind

The Steall Ruins below the Aonach Beag Massif

Route 2:

Dun Deardail Hill Fort

This easy walk climbs to the remains of an Iron Age hill fort, perched in a superb location overlooking Glen Nevis, with fantastic views for some distance in all directions. Historians can soak up the history contained within the partially vitrified stone blocks comprising the remains of the rampart, pondering as to what this fort once looked like and why it was deliberately destroyed. The views southward to the majority of the Mamores, as well as westward to Ben Nevis, are the best from any hill at such a lowly height, a mere 347m above sea level. Much of this walk involves easy walking along a wide Land Rover track forming the northernmost portion of the West Highland Way, a well-walked route which runs for 154km (96 miles) from Fort William all the way to Milngavie, on the north-western outskirts of Glasgow. This walk only takes a few hours and is ideal for families, with the potential to continue further along the West Highland Way as far as time or weather permit.

Dun Deardail Hill Fort	
Difficulty	**Very Easy**
Distance	**8.4 km (5.2 miles)**
Cumulative ascent	**320m**
Approximate time taken	**2-3 hours**
Munros	-
Subsidiary Tops	-
Advisories	• Midges can be bad in summer • Short steep ascent up a muddy path to the hill fort

Route 2 Summary

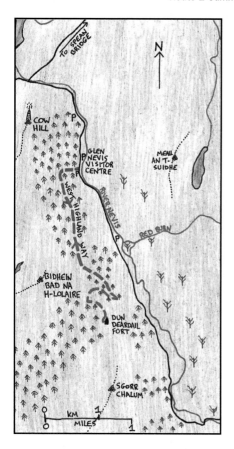

Route 2 Sketch Map

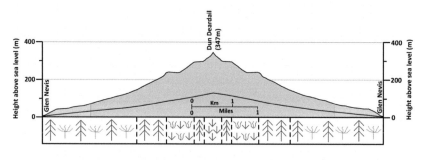

Route 2 Walk Profile

The route starts at a path signposted for the West Highland Way, off the main road through Glen Nevis. The car can either be parked at the Glen Nevis Visitor Centre car park, where a fee is charged for parking, or at a layby along the road almost adjacent to the start of the walk. Follow the path westward for 300m, as it leads into a short section of coniferous forest and climbs to meet a well-made Land Rover track, contouring along the steep slopes just above Glen Nevis. A wooden signpost indicates that walkers should turn left here and follow the track south to south-eastward for Dun Deardail, whilst a small path starting behind the sign marks the start of the climb towards Cow Hill (**Route 3**).

This track, part of the West Highland Way, contours above Glen Nevis at a nearly level gradient through open mixed coniferous and deciduous (predominantly silver birch and alder) forest. Bear right where the track splits after 550m, to commence a long but relatively gentle climb up the western slopes of Glen Nevis. Frequent gaps in the open forest cover allow fantastic views across the glen to the mighty bulks of Ben Nevis and Meall an t-Suidhe. Five Finger Gulley looks particularly spectacular between the summit plateau of Ben Nevis and its SW Top Carn Dearg, the location of a number of fatal accidents over the years, as the main Mountain Track passes fairly close to the top of the corrie. Meanwhile to the south, the western Mamores of Sgurr a' Mhaim and Stob Ban rise impressively high above Glen Nevis Forest in the foreground.

Following a more level section, the track starts to rise again south-eastward into thicker coniferous forest before turning abruptly north-westward at a hairpin bend to climb at more of a moderate gradient. The path soon rises out of the forest, with heathery, grassy and partially-forested slopes rising southward to An Dun, a lower hill obscuring the higher grassy hillock sporting the Dun Deardail Hill Fort beyond. The track abruptly turns south-westward at another hairpin bend to climb towards another dense pine plantation. Just before entering this pine forest, however, a small but well-built path signposted for Dun Deardail leads off eastward, skirting along the northern margin of this plantation. At the start of this path, an information post summarises and illustrates what is known about the fascinating history of the Dun Deardail Hill Fort. Follow the path eastward then south-eastward to climb to the base of the steep-sided hill on which the fort was constructed. The path splits here, with the best option to bear right and slant up the steep muddy north-western slopes, to enter the ruins of the fort through the former entrance.

The Dun Deardail Hill Fort is perched in a spectacularly exposed commanding location at the crest of a grassy pinnacle, a fantastic lookout post for an approaching army from any direction. Stone blocks forming the ancient rampart still rim the hill top; however these are now partially or completely overgrown by grass. This pinnacle offers awesome views along the River Nevis, a classic braided river system flowing away northward through fertile Glen Nevis towards Loch Linnhe. The immense western slopes of Ben Nevis rise up impressively across the opposite side of the glen, with steep vegetated lower slopes soaring upward to a complex system of crags and buttresses supporting the summit plateau, along with the mountain's neighbouring SW Top Carn Dearg.

The Allt Coire Ghaimhnean crashes down from a source high up in Five Finger Gulley, dividing into a number of distributary channels and forming a vast triangular-shaped alluvial fan as the gradient levels out in Glen Nevis, forcing the River Nevis to kink west around this vast cone of vegetated rock debris. The Red Burn cuts deeply into the mountain face between Ben Nevis and Meall an t-Suidhe, the latter almost dwarfed into insignificance by the extraordinary bulk of the former. Meanwhile to the south many of the Mamores poke up, from Binnein Mor in the east to Mullach nan Coirean in the west. Sgurr a' Mhaim is particularly prominent along the southern margin of the glen, it's long and steep NW ridge reaching out towards you and representing an arduous descent from the Ring of Steall (**Route 15**). The north ridge of Stob Ban appears a far more difficult prospect, with some steep and narrow rock faces towards the top. The triangular granite mass of Mullach nan Coirean pokes up to the right-hand side of Sgorr Chalum, the rounded hill whose rough grassy, heathery and bouldery slopes rise up in the foreground. This is indeed a fine spot, so take some time to savour and enjoy the views.

Dun Deardail is thought to have been built about 2000 years ago during the Iron Age, at one time potentially forming a real focal point within the glen, impressive flags flying high and visible from throughout lower Glen Nevis and as far afield as the Great Glen. The fort may have been occupied by different tribes at different times, as well as being rebuilt on several occasions during its existence. Much is still unknown about what exactly went on here however, with many attractive images of how the fort may have looked like being little more than imagination or speculation. A recent archaeological survey revealed that the fort occupies an area of about 1250m^2, is oriented NE-SW and roughly droplet-shaped in plan view, narrowing to its north-eastern end. There is strong evidence that the fort was abruptly destroyed by deliberate fire, perhaps by a rival tribe, as many of the remaining stones comprising the rampart reveal evidence of being partially melted (vitrified). Such intense heat could only be generated by significant stoking of the fire through the application of significant additional material to burn.

Alternatives

Given sufficient time, it is possible to continue further along the wide Land Rover track of the West Highland Way into the desolate pass of the Lairig, between the steep slopes of Meall a' Chaorainn and Doire Ban. The Allt na Lairige Moire meanders serenely northward through a wide open U-shaped valley here, as the West Highland Way clings to the lower western slopes of Meall a' Chaorainn. The pass is particularly beautiful in autumn, when the vegetation turns from the vivid green of summer to a spectacular russet brown colour. Return via the outbound route.

Ben Nevis from Dun Deardail

The Mamores from
Dun Deardail

95

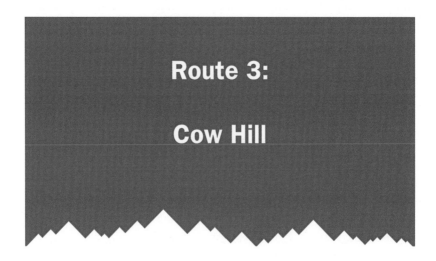

Route 3:

Cow Hill

Cow Hill is the distinctive forested hill rising abruptly to the east and south-east of Fort William town centre, sporting a rather unsightly large communications mast at the summit. Despite the obtrusive mast, the rounded summit is a very rewarding viewpoint across much of the adjacent town, as well as across Loch Linnhe and Loch Eil to the neighbouring towns of Corpach, Caol and Banavie. The hill's name is derived from the tradition of grazing cattle in the area, and highland cattle are commonly encountered around the summit of Cow Hill today. This route involves a steep climb up from Glen Nevis, through mixed coniferous-deciduous forest which is home to pine martens and roe deer, representing a rare opportunity to spot these shy animals. A network of other tracks wind their way around the summit, including the "Cow Hill Circuit", with the potential to make an easy full day out on the hill.

Cow Hill	
Difficulty	Very Easy
Distance	5.6 km (3.4 miles)
Cumulative ascent	310m
Approximate time taken	2-3 hours
Munros	-
Subsidiary Tops	Cow Hill (287m)
Advisories	• Midges can be bad in summer • Steep ascent up the western slopes of Glen Nevis

Route 3 Summary

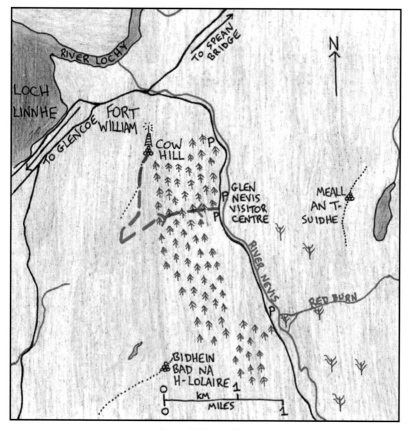

Route 3 Sketch Map

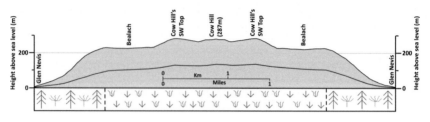

Route 3 Walk Profile

The walk starts, as for the Dun Deardail Hill Fort, at a path signposted for the West Highland Way, off the main road through Glen Nevis. Follow the path westward for 300m, as it climbs through a short section of coniferous forest to meet a well-made Land Rover track, contouring along the steep slopes just above Glen Nevis. Instead of turning left here for Dun Deardail (**Route 2**), cross this Land Rover track and locate a small path on the opposite side, signposted for Cow Hill.

This well-built path climbs away steeply up the western margin of Glen Nevis, through a pleasant mixture of coniferous and deciduous (predominantly silver birch and alder) forest. Despite several short zigzags, this section is tiring as the path climbs 160m in height over 700m distance, to abruptly emerge from the forest at a fence and a metal gate. The tall digital TV mast on Cow Hill now pokes up to the north, high above the northern slopes of Cow Hill's SW Top. A small path darts off right here, descending gently northward into coniferous forest, marked by a wooden post with an orange band and seemingly heading in roughly the right direction for the summit of Cow Hill. However this path gradually descends to contour across the hill's forested eastern and northern slopes, without offering a route to the summit. Instead pass through the metal gate on a track marked by a wooden post with a yellow band, which appears to initially head in the wrong direction for Cow Hill. The path leads south-westward through open heathery and grassy countryside, across the boggy col below Cow Hill's SW Top, to connect with a wide track carving its way across Cow Hill's southern slopes. Turn right (north) here, marked by a wooden post with a black band, to climb up the eastern slopes of Cow Hill's SW Top, bypassing the summit and crossing a stile. Descend gently to a col below Cow Hill, then climb easily on the Land Rover track to the rounded open grassy and heathery summit, dominated by the huge digital TV mast in the centre.

The best views from Cow Hill are attained from the margins of the rounded summit. By heading past the mast on a muddy path to the western margin, there are fine views across Fort William, lying directly beneath the hill's western slopes, as well as across Loch Linnhe, Loch Eil and the hills to the north of Loch Eil and Glenfinnan. From the actual summit to the south of the mast, there are equally fine views eastward and southward to the immense bulk of the Ben Nevis Massif, as well as the western Mamores from Sgurr a' Mhaim to Mullach nan Coirean. Highland cattle traditionally grazed the slopes and summit of Cow Hill until 2003, then were temporarily removed, until being returned to the hill again in 2011. These animals are frequently encountered by walkers and help to keep the vegetation in check, creating the ideal habitat for Black Grouse and other wild birds. Return via the outbound route, taking care down the steep descent back to Glen Nevis.

Alternatives

To make a full day out on the hill, after climbing to the top why not walk the remaining 4.9km (3 miles) of the "Cow Hill Circuit", an easy route encircling the summit. After descending back to the col below Cow Hill's SW Top, follow the yellow waymark posts to descend towards Fort William, then contour around the hill's lower forested slopes back to the start of the West Highland Way in Glen Nevis. Turn left here and descend back to the start of the walk.

Panorama looking west from Cow Hill to Fort William and Corpach

Ben Nevis, Sgurr a' Mhaim and Stob Ban (left to right) from Cow Hill

Route 4:

Charles Inglis Clark (CIC) Hut and Coire Leis

This fine walk into the glen of the Allt a' Mhuilinn offers an opportunity to gaze up in awe at the magnificent North Face of Ben Nevis, the mountain's most spectacular feature and one which walkers up the "Mountain Track" can never fully appreciate. This hike is ideal for a day with less than perfect weather, when the clouds are down on the higher Munros, but still involves a significant amount of climbing, so it could be used as a warm up for major Munro expeditions in the coming days. This walk is understandably very popular in good weather throughout the year, with the more adventurous combining this route with an ascent of Ben Nevis or Carn Mor Dearg. But beware of doing this walk if heavy rain or showers are forecast. Coire Leis is one of the wettest corries in the Highlands, catching the worst of the weather tracking across the neighbouring high summits of Ben Nevis and Carn Mor Dearg.

Charles Inglis Clark (CIC) Hut and Coire Leis	
Difficulty	Easy
Distance	10.6 km (6.6 miles)
Cumulative ascent	620m
Approximate time taken	3-5 hours
Munros	-
Subsidiary Tops	-
Advisories	• Strong footwear essential • Path and terrain become increasingly wild and rocky around and beyond the CIC Hut • Steep gradient at times through Leanachan Forest early in the walk • Midges, horse flies and mosquitoes can be bad in summer close to the Allt a' Mhuilinn

Route 4 Summary

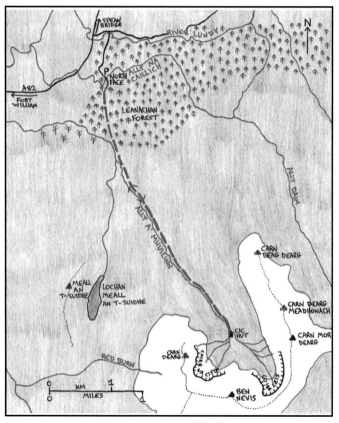

Route 4 Sketch Map

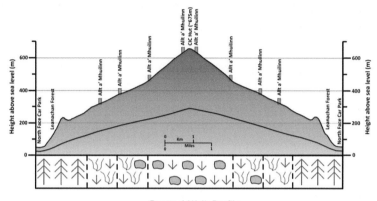

Route 4 Walk Profile

Leave the North Face car park, heading SE along a wide well-made track towards coniferous forest, crossing the Allt na Caillich on a wide concrete bridge. As the main track bends abruptly to the left (NE), a small stony path swings off to the right, climbing away southward along the edge of Leanachan Forest above the Fort William Golf Course, signposted for the Allt a' Mhuilinn and Ben Nevis access. Climb fairly steeply up this path for a short distance until a junction with a path running SW-NE is reached. Cross this small intersecting path and continue southward on a fairly modern path that rises into the dense heart of the coniferous Leanachan Forest, once again signposted for Ben Nevis. The path rises in several stages of quite steep ascent; however a number of park-type benches are situated at the side of the path at convenient points during the climb, should the steep sections be tiring early in the day. Occasional breaks in the tree cover allow fine views westward to the hills around Glenfinnan, as well as the small towns of Corpach and Banavie at the northern termination of Loch Linnhe, with conspicuous cliffs marking the nearby Banavie Quarry. In the midst of the final steep ascent, a signposted path leads away westward through the pine trees to a scenic viewpoint, the first sight of Ben Nevis in all its glory.

The incredibly steep, dull grey and scree-covered western slopes of the Ben rise to the top of Carn Dearg (Ben Nevis' NW Munro Top), then the vast summit plateau gradually rises southeastward to the broad summit of Ben Nevis itself. A complex system of solid andesite buttresses and frowning crags of the mountain's North Face glare incredulously at you, soaring high above the valley of the Allt a' Mhuilinn. A complete contrast to the steep yet smooth western and southern slopes of the mountain, and a contrast that walkers on the "Mountain Track" up from Achintee can never fully appreciate. It's easy to see from here how the mood of the mountain changes in tandem with the typically fickle Lochaber weather.

Return to the main path and after a further short section through dense forest, the path abruptly turns south-westward and emerges into more open countryside, bordered by pine forest only on the left (eastern) side. Continue on the path as it turns to the left (SE) and joins a wider stony track before reaching a stile. Beyond the stile, the small path enters wild countryside and the start of the hanging valley of the Allt a' Mhuilinn, already at almost 300 metres altitude.

The valley of the Allt a' Mhuilinn is a splendid example of a hanging U-shaped valley, carved by the slow erosive action of a mountain glacier during the last glacial phase. Even more spectacular is the remote and rugged Coire Leis at the head of the valley, holding snow well into the summer months beneath precipitous granite cliffs and crags of the Carn Mor Dearg (CMD) Arête. Coire Leis receives some of the worst weather in the Highlands, with torrential rain, gale force icy winds and low cloud all too frequently battering the head of this wild corrie, along with neighbouring Ben Nevis and Carn Mor Dearg. Steep heathery slopes, partially blanketed by large granite blocks and pale red scree, rise to the rounded bouldery summit of Carn Beag Dearg and the pointed shapely beacons of Carn Dearg Meadhonach and Carn

Mor Dearg, appearing rather more rounded from this close proximity and forming the enclosing northern border of Coire Leis. The steep red slopes of Carn Mor Dearg's north ridge contrast starkly with the precipitous dark grey cliffs, crags and corries of Ben Nevis, forming the abrupt southern wall of the valley. Remote corries, crevasses and scree shoots, carved out of the crystalline volcanic bedrock by millennia of glacial activity, nestle into the cliffs. These often encompass thick banks of solid winter snow and ice throughout the year, especially during cold summers. Waterfalls and streams issue from the melting snow, feeding crystal clear suspended lochans nestling into the contours between rugged crags, accessible only to the well-equipped rock and ice climber.

With the use of a map, it is easy to visualise how this landscape looked about 13,000 years ago during the last glacial phase in Scotland. Hanging mountain glaciers suspended in Coire Leis and Coire Giubhsachan progressively carved back into the heads of their respective corries, underground ice streams efficiently carrying away the eroded rock flour and boulders, depositing this as glacial moraine surrounding and in front of the ice floe. As erosion continued, the watershed between the heads of the glaciers became thinner and thinner, sculpting out the delicate scythe-like CMD Arête, a pleasure for the mountaineer and rock climber during our current interglacial climatic state.

Continue SE up the path, with the foaming ice-cold waters of the Allt a' Mhuilinn crashing over and around angular granite blocks on the right-hand side. This path continues on up alongside the Allt a' Mhuilinn to the CIC Hut, beyond which the path becomes indistinct in the tight confines of wild upper Coire Leis. In this upper section, the terrain becomes increasingly wild and bouldery, situated directly beneath the frowning cliffs and crags supporting the summit of Ben Nevis. In good weather it is a common sight to see rock or ice climbing parties grouping at the base of Tower Ridge or Douglas Boulder, ready to attempt a precipitous climb to the summit, along with other parties picking their way painstakingly up the North Face high above them. Ben Nevis' North Face provides some of the best rock and ice climbs on the British mainland, and such pursuits are therefore popular in winter and summer alike.

The Charles Inglis Clark (CIC) Hut was constructed during 1928-1929 by a Dr. and Mrs. Inglis Clark as a memorial to their son Charles, who was killed in Mesopotamia in 1918, while fighting in the First World War. The hut was presented to the Scottish Mountaineering Club (SMC) by Charles' parents in 1929 and has been owned by the club ever since, being significantly extended and renovated during 2008-2012. The remote location of the hut resulted in difficult transport of building materials to the site. During initial construction in the late 1920s, building materials were transported arduously by pony-back, during the 2008-2012 renovation by helicopter. The hut is situated in a spectacular location beneath immense cliffs supporting the summit plateau of the Ben and is often used as a base for mountain climbers, predominantly those of the SMC. Continue into the wild and remote Coire Leis as far as time, weather or energy permit, and then return via the outbound route.

Looking west to Corpach, Banavie and Loch Eil from Leanachan Forest

Ben Nevis and Carn Mor Dearg from the viewpoint in Leanachan Forest

The Charles Inglis Clark (CIC) Hut

Route 5:

Meall an t-Suidhe

Meall an t-Suidhe, translating as "Hill of the Seat", is the rounded grassy hill that dominates the view to the south-east of Fort William. This hill obscures Ben Nevis when viewed from the north-eastern part of the town and is indeed often mistaken for the Ben itself, especially when the summit of Britain's highest mountain is concealed in a veil of cloud. Although only of Graham height, the ideal position of the hill high above Fort William and Loch Linnhe results in fine views to the west from the rounded summit, better than from the Ben itself due to closer proximity. This is very much the hill for a day when the clouds are down on the Munros, as owing to its lower altitude (just over half the height of Ben Nevis), the top of Meall an t-Suidhe is far more often beneath the cloud base. This hill could also represent an alternative for those who bail out of the climb up Ben Nevis, due to fatigue or deteriorating weather conditions, or as a warm-up climb in training for higher Munro expeditions in coming days.

Meall an t-Suidhe	
Difficulty	Easy
Distance	9 km (5.6 miles)
Cumulative ascent	700m
Approximate time taken	3-5 hours
Munros	-
Subsidiary Tops	Meall an t-Suidhe (711m)
Advisories	• Strong grippy footwear is essential • Rough and pathless slopes must be ascended to reach the summit cairn

Route 5 Summary

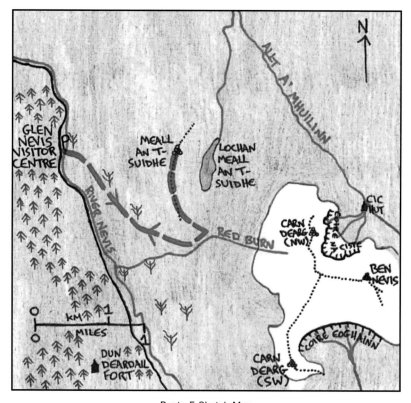

Route 5 Sketch Map

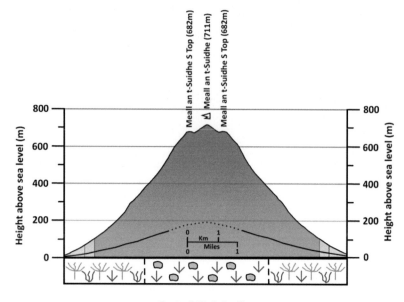

Route 5 Walk Profile

The walk starts, as for the climb up Ben Nevis via the Mountain Track, in the Glen Nevis Visitor Centre car park, where a fee is charged for parking. Alternatively, the walk can be started from the Glen Nevis Youth Hostel (0.9 miles further south down Glen Nevis), from where a track heads ENE to join the main Mountain Track from the Visitor Centre higher up the steep western slopes of Meall an t-Suidhe.

From the Visitor Centre, head towards the northern end of the car park to locate a metal suspension bridge across the River Nevis, which sways as walkers cross much like a boat on a choppy sea. Once across, follow the dirt path southward through the trees past Achintee House, until the main path turns abruptly to the left (east), and starts to progressively climb directly towards the steep grassy slopes of Meall an t-Suidhe. At the end of this short section, cross a stile and continue a few more steps eastward to a large well-built cairn, before taking a sharp right onto the main "Mountain Track" for Ben Nevis. The Mountain Track then slants south-eastward up the steep slopes of Meall an t-Suidhe and soon becomes rocky with the necessity for good footwear. The gradient gradually steepens as the track rounds the western then southern slopes of Meall an t-Suidhe, involving a couple of short zigzags and fording a number of small burns on metal and wooden bridges. Glen Nevis gradually drops away beneath you, whilst to the south the western Mamores of Sgurr a' Mhaim, Stob Ban and Mullach nan Coirean look impressive.

One of the steepest sections is reached as the path turns NE across the south-eastern slopes of Meall an t-Suidhe high above the Red Burn, which crashes through a rocky valley beneath you. Above this steep section, the path swings abruptly to the WSW for a short section before swinging back towards the NE. The main path should be vacated as it swings to the NE, as you are in closest proximity here to the South Top of Meall an t-Suidhe, who's grassy and boggy slopes rise above to the NW.

Cross a small burn, representing a minor outflow from the head of Lochan Meall an t-Suidhe, then ascend the rough, grassy, intermittently boggy and pathless slopes, with scattered granite boulders, to reach the South Top of Meall an t-Suidhe (682m). These slopes are steep for a time, but the gradient starts to level off as the South Top is approached. It is a good idea to keep to the highest ground in order to avoid the worst of the boggy sections. The view suddenly opens up to the west, with the long body of Loch Linnhe leading south-westward towards the Atlantic Ocean. Follow the wide ridge northward as it descends to a narrow col, then makes the final rise up a mixture of grass and granite boulders, still boggy in places, to the rounded cairned summit of Meall an t-Suidhe (711m).

From the summit, now high above the desolate water body of Lochan Meall an t-Suidhe, the Mountain Track appears to carve a conspicuous tramline through the steep grey andesite screes of the Ben Nevis Massif. This track is often lined with trains of ant-like walkers, much like a busy motorway facilitating a quick and convenient transport route to the summit of Britain's highest mountain. By contrast, few walkers make the trudge to Meall an t-Suidhe and it is quite easy to enjoy the summit to yourself. The vast western slopes of Ben Nevis, whilst not the most attractive feature of the mountain, are spectacularly reflected in the still waters of Lochan Meall an t-Suidhe on a calm day. The pointed summits of Carn Mor Dearg and Sgurr a' Mhaim flank the Ben Nevis Massif to the left and right respectively. To the west, the view down the lengths of Loch Linnhe, Loch Eil and across the sea of mountains approaching the Scottish west coast is very photogenic. Fort William is out of sight from the summit cairn, and the best views to the west and east are gained from the margins of the rounded summit.

Return via the outbound route, back southward along the crest of the wide ridge. Descend SE from the South Top to pick up the Mountain Track at the apex of its zigzag, followed by a long descent back to the Glen Nevis Visitor Centre or Youth Hostel.

Ben Nevis from Meall an t-Suidhe in late autumn

Panorama westward to Fort William, Loch Linnhe and Loch Eil from Meall an t-Suidhe

Late afternoon sunshine casts rays through the mist onto the Dun Deardail Hill Fort, with Mullach nan Coirean and Stob Ban to the left

Route 6:

Coire Giubhsachan

The valley of the Allt Coire Guibhsachan, with Coire Giubhsachan at its head, is one of the best examples of a glacially scoured U-shaped valley in the area and a mecca for glacial sedimentologists. The preserved terminal moraine and erratic boulders are easily identifiable at the foot of the valley, providing a fantastic depiction of how the valley was carved by the erosive action of ice up to about 13,000 years ago. The valley wanderer will be happy to potter around at the foot of the valley, enjoying a paddle in the gently meandering burn, or searching for gems which sparkle in abundance on the river bed beneath the crystal-clear ice-cold water. Meanwhile, the more adventurous will pick their way into increasingly rough terrain as they climb to the grassy bealach at the head of the corrie, to enjoy a fantastic view down two opposing U-shaped valleys from a high watershed at 830m. Coire Giubhsachan is fairly secluded and poorly frequented by walkers, most of which pass through quickly on their way to climbing the lofty summits of Carn Mor Dearg or the Aonachs. Therefore this corrie is a perfect place for solitude, under favourable weather conditions forming a superb sun trap beneath the mighty slopes of Aonach Beag and the CMD Arête, whilst at other times holding winter's icy grip firmly in its grasp.

Coire Giubhsachan	
Difficulty	Easy
Distance	7.4 km (4.6 miles) return to entrance of Coire Giubhsachan, 12.4 km (7.8 miles) return to bealach with Carn Mor Dearg
Cumulative ascent	360m to entrance of Coire Giubhsachan, 700m to bealach with Carn Mor Dearg
Approximate time taken	2-3 hours return to entrance of Coire Giubhsachan, 4-5 hours return to bealach with Carn Mor Dearg
Munros	-
Subsidiary Tops	-
Advisories	• Strong, grippy and waterproof footwear essential • Boggy sections in the Steall Meadows and foot of Coire Giubhsachan • Steep final ascent to the bealach with Carn Mor Dearg • Midges, horse flies and mosquitoes can be bad in summer

Route 6 Summary

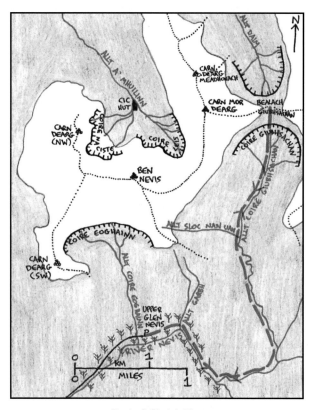

Route 6 Sketch Map

115

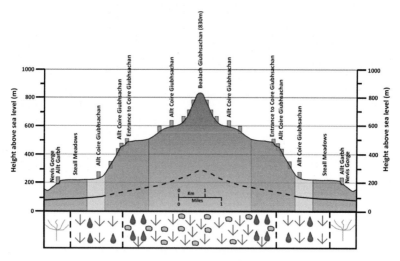

Route 6 Walk Profile

Glen Nevis to the entrance of Coire Giubhsachan

Starting in the popular car park at the road end in Glen Nevis, take the path leading eastward into the tight confines of the Nevis Gorge, before emerging into the attractive Steall Meadows with a fantastic view of the Steall Waterfall. Follow the occasionally muddy path adjacent to the River Nevis until a wooden bridge fording the Allt Coire Giubhsachan is reached, just before Steall Ruins.

Leave the main path through Glen Nevis just before the bridge and ascend to gain a narrow, rough and broken path, climbing steeply up the hillside in close proximity to the Allt Coire Giubhsachan; an impressive river that cascades down the steep hillside in a series of foaming waterfalls. Height is soon gained above Glen Nevis and the panorama opens up, taking in the central and eastern Mamores, from Binnein Beag to Sgurr a' Mhaim. Keep

116

to the path as these slopes can be very boggy, confirmed by the abundance of cotton grass on the adjacent hillside. Even the path itself can turn into a mini torrent during or immediately after heavy rainfall, so waterproof boots are essential for this section. Higher up the gradient temporarily slackens, with the grey hump of Ben Nevis, curving line of the Carn Mor Dearg (CMD) Arête, and pointed beacon of Carn Mor Dearg popping into view. A final steep climb terminates at the entrance to Coire Giubhsachan, and the path levels out immediately adjacent to the Allt Coire Giubhsachan at this point.

Coire Giubhsachan is a splendid example of a hanging U-shaped valley, scoured by erosion from a mountain glacier during the last glacial phase some 13,000 years ago. The impenetrable walls of the CMD Arête enclose the valley to the NW, a mixture of grassy and sheer rock faces of damp mossy granite, from which issue numerous foaming watery cascades, plummeting vertically down the hillside to the peacefully meandering Allt Coire Giubhsachan far below. The steep grassy, then higher up craggy, western slopes of Aonach Beag tower up to the east, whilst to the south the Mamores of An Gearanach and Binnein Mor stand bold on the opposite side of tranquil Glen Nevis. A band of hummocky topography at the foot of the hanging valley represents the preserved vegetated artefact of the terminal moraine, which formed at the foot of the former glacier and records its maximum advance down the valley. Large scattered blocks of striated schist, sporadically distributed across this hummocky terrain, represent erratic boulders carried down the valley by the former glacier and dumped once the ice melted. Some of these blocks are precariously perched on hillocks, with their transport to such a location seemingly impossible by wind or water, invoking ice as the primary transport mechanism.

Continuing up Coire Giubhsachan to the bealach with Carn Mor Dearg (830m)

Continue NW along the path, which becomes indistinct but temporarily leaves the Allt Coire Giubhsachan and heads directly for the walls of the CMD Arête across extremely boggy terrain. Alternatively one could follow the bank of the Allt Coire Giubhsachan, which meanders peacefully and serenely across the low boggy gradient; quartz, mica and feldspar derived from erosion of the prevailing granites upstream sparkle like jewels beneath the crystal clear, ice-cold waters. This is indeed a fine spot for a paddle on a hot day, rather more secluded than along the shore of the River Nevis. The gradient progressively steepens further up Coire Giubhsachan, several streams draining the steep south-eastern walls of the CMD Arête are forded, and soon the path runs back adjacent to the Allt Coire Giubhsachan, which flows fast and efficiently over smooth polished flags of red granite. The terrain becomes increasingly rough up the valley and the walls of the Arête loom closer and closer, looking slightly less impenetrable than before.

The final steep slog up the head of Coire Giubhsachan to the bealach at 830m is tiring, as the path climbs steeply in steps hewn out of peat and granite sand, on the left (western) bank of the Allt Coire Giubhsachan. Finally the steep slope abruptly eases off and the boggy Bealach Giubhsachan between Carn Mor Dearg and Aonach Mor is attained, complete with several small pools and scattered granite blocks set amongst lush green grass. This is a fine vantage point to admire the view northward down the bleak U-shaped valley of the Allt Daim, between the north ridge of Carn Mor Dearg and the immense gullied western slopes of Aonach Mor. Numerous alluvial fans cascade down the steep lower slopes of the latter, derived from rocky outcrops higher up the mountain. Meanwhile to the south there is a fine view down much of the length of the beautiful Coire Giubhsachan, the outer portion of which curves round out of view behind Aonach Beag's SW ridge. Descend via the outbound route, back through Coire Giubhsachan, Steall Meadows and the Nevis Gorge to reach the car park at the road end, taking about 2 hours from the bealach.

Ben Nevis, Carn Mor Dearg and the CMD Arête from the entrance to Coire Giubhsachan

Binnein Beag, Binnein Mor, Na Gruagaichean, An Gearanach and Stob Coire a' Chairn (left to right) from the entrance to Coire Giubhsachan

Looking down through Coire Giubhsachan to the Ring of Steall and Stob Ban

Carn Mor Dearg and Carn Dearg Meadhonach from Bealach Giubhsachan

Route 7:

The summits and ridges of the Mullach nan Coirean Massif

Mullach nan Coirean is one of the easier Munros in the Mamore Range and amongst the most ideal for beginners, or those that are new to the area. Not only is it the lowest Munro summit described in this book, it is easily accessed from the road through Glen Nevis, which conveniently passes by the base of the mountain. Having said that, no Munro summit in this area is "easy", with the climb of Mullach nan Coirean still including the customary sections of steep ascent and rough rocky terrain near the top. This route also includes an optional easy walk out to the neighbouring Top of Meall a' Chaorainn, which offers a fantastic view down the length of Loch Linnhe and an ideal opportunity to explore this spectacular granite topography. Mullach nan Coirean and the western portion of Meall a' Chaorainn are actually composed of two distinct granite complexes, separated by a belt of schist, but both were intruded about 400 million years ago at the end of the Caledonian Orogeny. Mullach nan Coirean is an attractive mountain and this route can be taken at an easier pace to make a fine day out, providing a good introduction to walking the Munros of the Mamore Range.

The summits & ridges of the Mullach nan Coirean Massif	
Difficulty	Medium
Distance	11.8 km (7.3 miles)
Cumulative ascent	980m
Approximate time taken	5-6 hours
Munros	Mullach nan Coirean (939m)
Subsidiary Tops	Meall a' Chaorainn (910m)
Advisories	• Some sections of steep and rough ascent/descent • Several boggy areas • Fairly narrow and rocky section near the top of Mullach nan Coirean's NE ridge, requiring specialist equipment when under snow/ice and unsuitable during high winds

Route 7 Summary

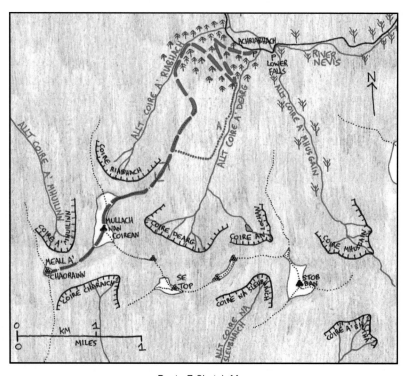

Route 7 Sketch Map

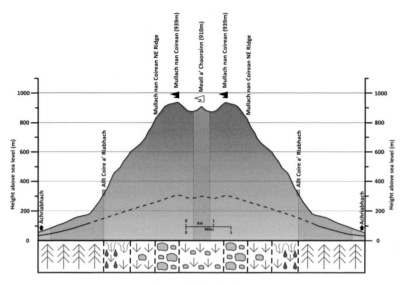

Route 7 Walk Profile

The route starts from Achriabhach, on the opposite side of the road to a row of small white cottages and about 250m (0.16 miles) west of the Lower Falls car park in Glen Nevis. The car can either be left at Achriabhach, where there is some space for off-road parking, or at the Lower Falls car park where a fee is charged. Take the well-made track leading westward from Achriabhach into coniferous forest through a metal gate. This Land Rover track climbs at a gentle gradient, with occasional breaks in the tree cover allowing fine views across to the immense bulk of Carn Dearg (Ben Nevis' SW Top) and down Glen Nevis, which starts to drop away beneath you.

There is a small network of different Land Rover tracks across the forested lower slopes of Mullach nan Coirean, and it is important to follow the right tracks to reach the base of the mountain's NE ridge, the standard ascent route from the north. From Achriabhach, climb WNW up the track for just over 0.5km (0.3

miles) until a junction is reached. Turn abruptly left here, and take the Land Rover track which sharply bends round to climb gently south-eastward. Follow this track for about 0.6 km (0.37 miles) until an abrupt hairpin. At the apex of this hairpin, a small path disappears off southward into dense vegetation, indicated by a small cairn. This path heads into Coire Dheirg, a large corrie enclosed by the NE ridge of Mullach nan Coirean and the N ridge of Stob Ban. The NE ridge can be attained via this route (Option A on the map); involving a very steep climb out of Coire Dheirg next to a deer fence (this is also a possible alternative for the descent). However the easiest route involves following the track as it swings sharply back north-westward and continues to climb through coniferous forest.

Another junction is reached after about 0.3km (0.19 miles), where a track swings off abruptly to the left and turns south-eastward to head into Coire Dheirg. This track joins the small path mentioned earlier, but the best route continues straight ahead north-westward for a further 0.4 km (0.25 miles), to where the pine forest has recently been felled. Near the apex of a gradual bend in the track, a small but well-made modern path branches off to the left and starts to climb fairly steeply through a litter of pine stumps and branches. Higher up, the path runs through a short section of open birch forest, before crossing a stile to emerge into open heathery countryside at the base of Mullach nan Coirean's NE ridge. Water can be collected at this point by descending a little to the right (west) adjacent to a fence, to reach the Allt Coire a' Riabhach.

From the stile, Mullach nan Coirean appears as a broad triangular mass, a large open rocky corrie beneath the summit enclosed like two restraining arms by the mountain's NE and N ridges. This watershed is drained by the Allt Coire a' Riabhach, which crashes down to a confluence with the River Nevis about 0.5km (0.3 miles) NW of Achriabhach. The NE ridge initially rises very steeply away southward, before curving south-westward and finally westward at a comparatively easier gradient to reach the fairly extensive granite summit plateau of the Mullach. The base of the NE ridge is perennially wet and extremely boggy, especially so after recent rainfall. This area forms a sump where water draining from the mountain's NE face collects on a slack gradient.

The broken path, now very rough and comprising loose and slippery scree in places, climbs very steeply up the lower section of the NE ridge through a mixture of heather, grass and scattered granite boulders, adjacent to a large deer fence on the left. This is the steepest climb of the day and height is soon gained above the stile and sump at the base of the ridge. The steep climb terminates at a shallow boggy depression, where planks of wood and poles have been lodged in the waterlogged ground to help cross the wettest sections. The small path then climbs at a much gentler gradient south-westward, along or on the north-western limb of the wide ridge crest. After about 0.5km (0.3 miles), the deer fence on the left abruptly turns 90° and descends very steeply into Coire Dheirg, where the alternative route rises to gain the crest of the NE ridge. Shortly after this point, the gradient starts to steepen again as the final climb is made towards the summit. The upper section of the NE ridge narrows attractively and becomes increasingly rough and rocky, with red granite crags guarding steep drops into Coire Dheirg on the left (south) side. Care should be taken across this final section during high winds or when coated in snow/ice, however it should present few problems under good summer conditions. Pass the false summit at the top of the NE ridge (indicated by a small cairn), then contour south-west and then south around the rim of the summit plateau above impressive cliffs at the head of Coire Dheirg, to reach the large granite tower-like cairn at the Munro summit (939m).

The summit of Mullach nan Coirean perhaps represents the best vantage point for the attractive mountains to the west of the Nevis Range, somewhat distant but stretching out towards the horizon across the opposite side of the wide open Great Glen. The blue waters of Loch Linnhe shimmer and stretch away south-westward towards the North Atlantic beyond the rounded summit of Meall a' Chaorainn, hidden behind the bulk of Mullach nan Coirean until this point. The Glencoe mountains rise up impressively south of the rounded summit plateau, with the pointed summits of Bidean nam Bian being particularly distinctive and recognisable at the western end of the range. Mullach nan Coirean is the westernmost Munro on the east-west trending Mamore Ridgeline, and there is a fine view eastward across the flat-topped summit of its SE Top, along an attractive red granite ridge to the steep quartzite screes of Stob Ban's western face. Beyond, the vast quartzite bulk of Sgurr a' Mhaim and the rugged crest of the Devil's Ridge dominate the scene, with the rounded summit of Sgurr an Iubhair, pointed summits of Na Gruagaichean and Am Bodach, and level summit ridge of Binnein Mor poking up to form an impressive backdrop. All of these are exciting mountains offering varying challenges to the mountain explorer and accessed via a variety of routes described in this book. Finally, across Glen Nevis to the north-east the bulks of the Nevis Range stand bold, the vast south-western slopes of the Ben Nevis Massif rising initially to Carn Dearg then up to the extensive summit plateau of Ben Nevis, beyond which the rounded summit of Aonach Beag and southern portion of Aonach Mor protrude out. The rugged glaciated valley of Glen Nevis narrows eastward into the tight confines of the Nevis Gorge, beyond which the pointed summits of the southern Grey Corries rise up.

To continue to Meall a' Chaorainn, descend SSW then SW from the summit cairn to pick up a small path which leads onto a wide grassy ridge. This ridge becomes asymmetrical as it narrows to a low point, with steep grassy slopes falling away to the north into the head of Coire a' Mhuilinn. From this low point, there is a fine view down the course of the Allt Coire a' Mhuilinn towards the open valley of the Great Glen and the northern termination of Loch

Linnhe. As the ridge starts to rise once more, the attractive red granites of Mullach nan Coirean are replaced by grey schist, forming a short rocky section along the ridge crest. This schist forms a belt separating the smaller Meall a' Chaorainn granite complex from the larger Mullach nan Coirean complex, and comprises the bedrock for the remainder of the ridge to the summit of Meall a' Chaorainn. The short rocky section is easily circumvented by a path on the southern side of the ridge crest, after which the ridge becomes grassy again and widens, as it rises gently westward to the large cairn at the rounded summit of Meall a' Chaorainn. This mountain, standing at 910m and a mere 4m below Munro level (914m), is the final peak at the western termination of the main east-west trending Mamore Ridgeline. Situated closer to Loch Linnhe than any other peak in the Mamore Range, the summit offers fine views down the length of the sea loch towards the North Atlantic. The rounded red granite bulk of Mullach nan Coirean rises to the north-east, beyond which the steep grey south-western slopes of Ben Nevis rise high in the background. The red granites of the Meall a' Chaorainn complex comprise the western slopes of the mountain, immediately west of the summit.

To return to Achriabhach, retrace the outbound route back over Mullach nan Coirean and down its NE ridge. For extra variety, it is possible to descend very steeply off the NE ridge into Coire Dheirg where the deer fence joins from the right (south), however the easiest descent method involves descending via the ascent route described here. Once down at the Land Rover track, remember to bear left at the first junction and then right at the second junction, to arrive back at Achriabhach through the metal gate.

Alternatives

From the summit of Mullach nan Coirean, a pleasant easy stroll can also be made along the wide grassy Mamore Ridgeline to the summit of the Mullach's SE Top (917m), or further east to a number of unnamed Tops along a rockier section of the ridge. The best method of descent is still down the Mullach's NE ridge, as descending the north ridge of Stob Ban to Glen Nevis involves some tricky sections of exposed scrambling down steep rock faces.

Stob Ban from Mullach nan Coirean's NE ridge

The iced-up summit cairn on Mullach nan Coirean backed by the Glencoe mountains

Stob Ban and Sgurr a' Mhaim from Mullach nan Coirean's NE ridge in summer

Stob Ban and Sgurr a' Mhaim from Mullach nan Coirean's NE ridge in winter

The Nevis Range and cliffs above Coire Dheirg from Mullach nan Coirean in summer

The Nevis Range and cliffs above Coire Dheirg from Mullach nan Coirean in winter

Summer panorama eastward from Mullach nan Coirean across the Mamores

Winter panorama eastward from Mullach nan Coirean across the Mamores

Meall a' Chaorainn and Loch Linnhe from Mullach nan Coirean

A setting sun picks out the Nevis Range across the summit plateau
of Mullach nan Coirean

Route 8:

Beinn na Caillich and Mam na Gualainn

Beinn na Caillich and Mam na Gualainn form the two highest points on an E-W trending ridge, a vegetated wedge of schist and quartzite which rises abruptly and steeply above the tranquil waters of Loch Leven. This route forms a long circuit and makes a superb full day out, climbing the one Corbett in the Mamore Range along an easy grassy ridge. Mam na Gualainn translates as "Pass of the Shoulder" and ranks as number 168 out of the 221 Scottish Corbetts in terms of height, however it's eastern Top, Beinn na Caillich, is often considered as the more interesting mountain and offers the best views. The walk utilises one of the most interesting parts of the West Highland Way, with the benefit of starting and finishing on a well-made and easy-to-follow track. These two mountains are infrequently climbed, very much overshadowed by the high Munros comprising the main backbone of the Mamore Range to the north. Nonetheless, these summits offer fine views in their own right, especially down the valley of the River Leven, across Loch Leven to the Aonach Eagach, and beyond Loch Linnhe to the Scottish west coast.

Beinn na Caillich and Mam na Gualainn	
Difficulty	Medium
Distance	19.1 km (11.9 miles)
Cumulative ascent	1,030m
Approximate time taken	7-9 hours
Munros	-
Corbetts	Mam na Gualainn (796m)
Subsidiary Tops	Beinn na Caillich (764m)
Advisories	• Long distance • Steep ascent up Beinn na Caillich • Boggy sections along the Beinn na Caillich-Mam na Gualainn ridge • Steep descent down rough pathless slopes off Mam na Gualainn

Route 8 Summary

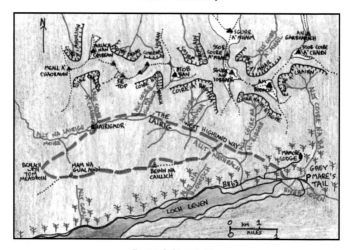

Route 8 Sketch Map

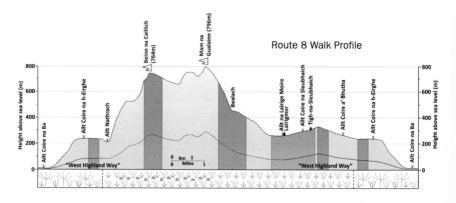

Route 8 Walk Profile

Starting at the Grey Mare's Tail Waterfall car park in the north of Kinlochleven, walk along the street north-westward, before bending round south-westward to join the main B863 road through the town. Cross the Allt Coire na Ba on the road bridge then walk about 200m westward on a pavement along the southern margin of the road, until a small stony path starts from the northern side, signposted for the West Highland Way and "Public Footpath to Fort William by the Lairig". The Lairig is the desolate pass between the western Mamores and the Beinn na Caillich-Mam na Gualainn ridge, used for the descent at the end of the walk.

This small rubbly path, comprising blocks of schist, quartzite and granite, climbs away up the northern side of the Leven valley through open silver birch forest. The gradient is relatively gentle initially, as the path fords the Allt Coire an Eich and a couple of other small streams, before crossing the tarmac track leading up to Mamore Lodge from the B863. The path starts to climb more steeply past this tarmac track, involving a series of zigzags as it climbs out of the birch forest into open heathery and grassy topography, to meet the wide Land Rover track from Mamore Lodge as it contours along the southern slopes of Am Bodach.

Turn left here and keep on the track for about 900m, as it slants gently westward up the lower south-western slopes of Am Bodach and then the south-eastern slopes of Sgurr an Iubhair, crossing the Allt Coire na h-Eirghe on a wooden bridge. Beinn na Caillich rises up high to the west, steep slopes ascending in two stages to the summit. An obvious path zigzags up the first major climb, but it is easy to miss the descent point from the Land Rover track to reach this path. This point is marked by a tiny pile of rocks, barely worthy of "cairn" status, pretty much on directly the opposite side of the valley to where the path zigzags up the first major climb towards the mountain. A rough, muddy path descends the heathery hillside and passes under some power lines, then crosses the Allt Nathrach via a wooden bridge. This river represents the final chance to fill up

135

with water before the Allt na Lairige Moire is forded, following the descent from Mam na Gualainn towards the end of the day, therefore water bottles should be filled here.

Now the climbing really starts, as the path progressively climbs then zigzags up the steep heathery slopes between some crags, to gain the eastern end of the ridge comprising Beinn na Caillich and Mam na Gualainn. Above this first steep section, the gradient levels out and the rough path leads along a wide ridge crest offering fine views southward to the pinnacled crest of the Aonach Eagach, eastward down the Leven valley, and northward to the dramatic Munro summits of the Mamores.

The final ascent to the first summit of Beinn na Caillich rises straight ahead, very steep heathery and bouldery slopes guarded higher up by a series of schistose crags. Therefore it is important to locate and keep to the correct path for safe navigation of this steep ascent, as veering off the path involves tough going. Bear right where the path splits shortly before the steep climbing starts, to veer westward then north-westward up the steep slopes. The path briefly zigzags higher up as it threads its way safely between the crumbling schistose crags, before curving along the upper north-eastern slopes of the mountain high above a remote lochan. The path finally bends southward to climb to the crest of the summit ridge, between the summit cairn of Beinn na Caillich (764m) and its eastern cairned Top.

It is worthwhile walking a few steps eastward to climb to the cairn on Beinn na Caillich's eastern Top, as this summit actually offers the best views, perched high above the mountain's steep eastern face. The panorama across the Leven valley, with the Mamores on one side and the Glencoe mountains on the other, is spectacular. The well-built Land Rover track of the West Highland Way carves a conspicuous scar along the lower slopes of the Mamores, in summer carrying countless walkers up from Glasgow to its final termination at Fort William. Meanwhile, the peaceful calm waters of Loch Leven fill the valley almost directly beneath your feet. From the summit of Beinn na Caillich itself, the onward route along the crest of an undulating but easy grassy ridge becomes apparent, descending to a low point before rising to a rounded unnamed Top, then up to the summit of Mam na Gualainn at the western termination of the ridge. Although just of Corbett height (764m, 2506ft), Beinn na Caillich is not considered as a separate mountain from the higher summit of Mam na Gualainn, therefore in the current standing is not a Corbett in its own right.

Follow the crest of the ridge as it descends in irregular fashion westward, involving easy walking across grass, patchy heather, and scattered blocks of schist, boggy in places. The northern slopes of the mountain curve away initially relatively gently from the crest of the ridge in a convex nature, whilst the southern slopes are comparatively steeper, plunging as a series of schistose cliffs and crags towards Loch Leven far below. Therefore it is wise to keep clear of the southern margin when snow-covered or in thick fog. The ridge descends to a narrow boggy col at 649m, where the path splits. The left-hand option bypasses the unnamed Top below Mam na Gualainn and contours along the steep southern slopes of the mountain, therefore walkers should bear right on a rough path to climb at a moderate gradient over blocks of quartzite to the unnamed Top at 755m. The attractive Loch an Sgoir nestles into the heathery contours just below the summit, with a number of other small lochans scattered across this boggy topography. Descend easily to another col before making a final moderately steep climb up the eastern slopes of Mam na Gualainn, with the slope gradient levelling off at the summit (796m).

Mam na Gualainn offers fine views westward across its neighbouring summit of Tom Meadhoin to Loch Linnhe and onwards to the Scottish west coast, as well as southward to the conical quartzite peak of Sgorr na Ciche (Pap of Glencoe) and the Aonach Eagach. There is a large cairn at the summit of Mam na Gualainn,

137

along with a cylindrical concrete trig point containing a plaque in memory of Royal Marines Reserve Anthony Callow. Anthony Callow, a keen mountain climber, was killed near Kinlochleven in 1997 at the age of 29. However it is unclear whether he died from a road accident, as was reported at the time, or during a military training exercise in the area using live ammunition.

The descent from Mam na Gualainn is long and rough. Unfortunately the northern slopes of the mountain are very steep and adorned by crags; therefore a quick descent back to the West Highland Way is not possible. Take a few steps north-west from the summit cairn to locate a deer fence and pick up a rough path adjacent to it, descending a grassy spur down the mountain's western slopes. Keep an eye out for a path on the opposite side of the fence and once this is spotted, climb over the fence and descend on this rough path. The path is muddy and boggy in places, becoming increasing indistinct and diffuse before fizzling out. From here descend the steep, rough, and boggy slopes westward towards the col with Tom Meadhoin. Lower down these slopes, it is possible to veer north or north-westward for a small shortcut, to intersect a rough rubbly path descending gently north-eastward across the north-western slopes of Mam na Gualainn from the col with Tom Meadhoin. This path actually represents an ancient route used to transport dead people for burial on an island called Eilean Munde, located in the western part of Loch Leven offshore from Ballachulish. There are fine views from this path up into the valley of the Allt na Lairige Moire, comprising the northern end of "the Lairig", between the granite summit of Meall a' Chaorainn and Doire Ban. The river meanders attractively through a wide and open U-shaped valley between the high heathery mountain slopes, which turn a striking russet brown colour in autumn.

The descent across Mam na Gualainn's lower northern slopes to the West Highland Way is relatively gentle, but long and relentless at this stage in the day. Several small streams are passed, followed by some power lines, before eventually the path emerges at the southern bank of the Allt na Lairige Moire. This river is relatively easy to ford when the water level is low, either by wading through in bare feet or using a series of rocks as stepping stones, but may prove very difficult to cross when in spate. If a crossing is not possible where the path intersects the river, head eastward along its southern bank, where further upstream the water plunges over numerous small waterfalls with more rocks to use as stepping stones. This is an attractive river, meandering and carving a course through pink granites of the Mullach nan Coirean complex. Once the river has been safely crossed, follow the path northward to the ruins at Lairigmor, where the path finally meets the track of the West Highland Way. The Lairigmor ruins actually represent the remains of a temporary shepherd's shelter; the blocks predominantly composed of pink Mullach nan Coirean granites, with scattered blocks of schist and quartzite thrown in for good measure.

The remainder of the descent now involves easy walking along the West Highland Way, through the desolate pass of the Lairig back to Kinlochleven. The easy Land Rover track gently rises eastward across the lower south-eastern slopes of Mullach nan Coirean, passing the unstable ruins of Tigh-na-sleubhaich ("The House of the Gullied Slope"), to reach the high point in the Lairig at an elevation of just over 330m. From here it is all downhill, following the track back to pick up the outbound route, then descending back to Kinlochleven.

Rising above the clouds over Loch Leven on the West Highland Way,
with Beinn na Caillich to the right

Above the sea of clouds across Loch Leven on the eastern slopes of Beinn na Caillich

A wintry shower encroaches on the valley of the Allt na Lairige Moire, viewed from the
north-western slopes of Mam na Gualainn in late autumn

Route 9:

Ben Nevis via the "Mountain Track"

The "Mountain Track" (also known as the "Tourist Track" or "Pony Track") is included here for completeness, being the easiest, fastest and comfortably the most popular route up Britain's highest mountain. The route follows a well-trodden path, however this is still a wild Munro. The path is very rough in places and the fickle Lochaber weather can change very suddenly with little warning, therefore proper mountain equipment, clothing and provisions are still very much required.

This is a serious mountain and too many walkers attempt this track unprepared for the conditions ahead. This is emphasised by the fact that around a quarter of the callouts received by the Lochaber Mountain Rescue Team, who assist with emergencies across a broad area from the Scottish islands to Creag Meagaidh, are to help with incidents on this path. The trail of litter and cigarette butts along the track tells a similar and disappointing story; this is a route used by the casual tourist to say they've "done it", and some of them probably shouldn't be subjecting their bodies to such extreme physical exertion at all.

Whilst it may be warm and sunny at the start of the day in Glen Nevis, walkers often ascend into thick fog and strong icy winds on the summit plateau of the Ben. Snow can fall on the summit at any time of year, even occasionally in July or August. There is no avoiding the fact that whichever route you choose, you will be starting from close to sea level, so the climb is long and strenuous. If you have little or no previous experience of Munro climbing then this is the best route for you, although a high level of fitness and stamina are still important pre-requisites for success.

For the more experienced and adventurous, a number of alternative routes to the summit of Ben Nevis are described in this book. These routes reveal aspects of the mountain that those climbing the Mountain Track can never fully appreciate, along with the opportunity to combine Britain's highest with some or all of the other exciting Munros in the Nevis Range.

Ben Nevis via the "Mountain Track"	
Difficulty	Medium
Distance	16 km (10 miles)
Cumulative ascent	1,330m
Approximate time taken	6-8 hours
Munros	Ben Nevis (1,344m)
Subsidiary Tops	-
Advisories	• Good level of fitness and stamina required • Strong grippy footwear and warm/waterproof clothing are essential • Excellent navigation and map-reading skills required on summit plateau when in dense fog or under snow/ice

Route 9 Summary

142

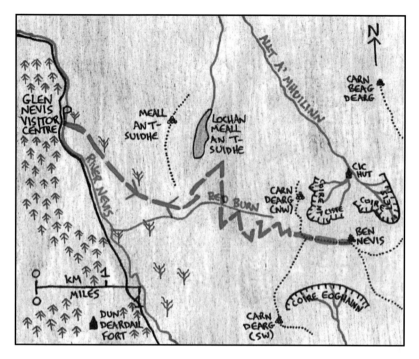

Route 9 Sketch Map

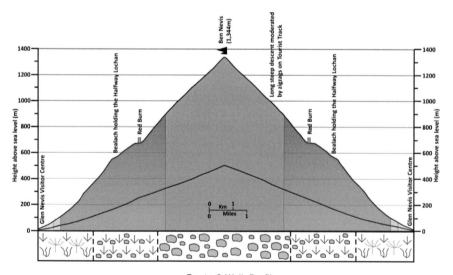

Route 9 Walk Profile

143

Most walkers start from the Glen Nevis Visitor Centre car park, where a fee is charged for parking. Information about Ben Nevis, along with the latest mountain weather forecast from the Met Office, is displayed within the visitor centre, both well worth a look before departing. Alternatively the walk can be started from the Glen Nevis Youth Hostel (about 1.5km [0.9 miles] further south down Glen Nevis), from where a track heads ENE to join the main Mountain Track from the Visitor Centre, higher up the steep western slopes of Meall an t-Suidhe.

Cross the River Nevis by a metal suspension bridge from the northern end of the Visitor Centre car park and follow the hordes of tourists southward on a well-used path, before turning eastward to ascend the lower slopes of Meall an t-Suidhe and reach the main Mountain Track for Ben Nevis. The Ben Nevis Inn is ideally located on the left here, which could make a convenient stop on the descent route to quench the thirst and celebrate the achievement (it is also possible to drive up to the inn from the north). It is probably not a good idea to stop at the pub on the way up if you plan to reach the summit! Turn right at a prominent cairn here and follow the Mountain Track as it slants south-eastward up the increasingly steep slopes of Meall an t-Suidhe, soon becoming rocky with the necessity for strong footwear.

One of the steepest sections is reached as the path veers NE across the high south-eastern slopes of Meall an t-Suidhe. It is here that walkers get the first real impression of the immense climb still to do up the grey andesite screes of Ben Nevis' western face, along with the realisation that the climbing so far has actually been up the mountain's neighbouring Top, Meall an t-Suidhe. Unsurprisingly it is at this point that those in high heels or ruined trainers or suffering from extreme fatigue get fazed and turn back.

Above this steep section, the path swings abruptly to the WSW for a short section before swinging back towards the NE, to climb to a large cairn above the desolate longitudinal water body of

Lochan Meall an t-Suidhe. This loch is nicknamed the "Halfway Lochan" as it allegedly represents the halfway point of the climb, although this is something of a misnomer as the loch actually lies at around 570m above sea level, less than half the height of Ben Nevis. The Mountain Track makes a sharp right turn at the cairn, whilst the path continuing north past the cairn leads into the glen of the Allt a' Mhuilinn and terminates at the CIC Hut, located in a spectacular location beneath precipitous cliffs and crags of the Ben's North Face.

After turning right at the cairn, the track ascends due south and soon cuts beneath an impressive waterfall formed by the Red Burn, representing a final opportunity to fill up water bottles before the summit is reached. From the Red Burn, the Mountain Track climbs the relentless western slopes of Ben Nevis via a series of broad zigzags. It is worthwhile keeping to the main path, as shortcutting the zigzags makes for tough going across steep, loose and slippery scree. Vegetation becomes increasingly scarce as height is gained and the upper slopes are almost entirely coated in monotonous grey andesite scree. Now high above the neighbouring hill of Meall an t-Suidhe and the Halfway Lochan, the view opens up to the west with a sea of mountains popping up all the way out towards the Scottish west coast.

The gradient eases off as the featureless summit plateau of Ben Nevis is reached. Five Finger Gulley cuts quite far into the summit plateau from the west and south, so care must be taken to not stray to the right (south or west) of the track, especially in fog or snow cover. The track erratically ascends across the plateau via a series of short rises. The most prominent of these is known as McLean's Steep (named after James McLean, who was contracted to build the Mountain Track as an access route to the Ben Nevis summit observatory in 1883), and often holds a large bank of iced winter snow until early July. Further on near the summit, the corries and gullies of the mountain's North Face cut quite far into the

145

plateau. The Mountain Track passes very close to Gardyloo Gulley in particular, which often holds large iced cornices well into July. These cornices overhang the northern cliffs, so you should not attempt to walk out onto them.

A series of large tower-like cairns have been constructed in recent years to highlight the route, very useful as a navigation aid when the plateau is snow-covered or in thick fog, but nonetheless completely destroying the wild feel of the mountain.

Shortly after Gardyloo Gulley, the summit of the UK's highest mountain is reached. The trig point sits atop an enormous summit cairn, with ruins of the hotel and observatory, numerous other memorials, hordes of proud walkers celebrating their achievement and sadly, often an unacceptable volume of litter. Please do not add to this.

The summit of Ben Nevis is reputedly shrouded in thick cloud 69% of the year; so some degree of fortune and careful scrutinizing of the weather forecast are essential to enjoy the privilege of the fine views from the top. The best views are actually from the margins of the plateau, rather than from the trig point near the centre. Approaching the northern margin of the plateau with care, the red north ridge of Carn Mor Dearg looks magnificent. The small pointed summits of Carn Beag Dearg (1010m), Carn Dearg Meadhonach (1179m) and Carn Mor Dearg (1220m) progressively rise towards the south; the western slopes bathed in red granite scree and looking impossibly steep from this vantage point.

Three ridges radiate from the pyramidal summit of Carn Mor Dearg: the easy north ridge connecting to Carn Dearg Meadhonach (**Route 13**), the exciting east ridge linking to Aonach Mor via the high Bealach Giubhsachan at 830m (**Route 14**, **Route 17**), and the delicate but spectacular CMD Arête, connecting to a steep boulder field beneath the summit of Ben Nevis (**Route 13**, **Route 14**, **Route 17**). The thin line of the CMD Arête departs from the summit of Carn Mor Dearg, then twists gracefully round the head of Coire Leis to disappear out of view below.

Far below in the heart of upper Coire Leis can be seen the CIC hut, recently extended and renovated, often used as a base for climbers of the SMC on numerous rock- or ice-climbing tours up the ridges of the Ben's North Face. Looking due east over the CMD Arête, the vast Aonach Ridge rises up, the steep grassy and gullied lower slopes soaring up to a series of rocky crags on Aonach Beag. Through the notch in the otherwise impenetrable Aonach Ridge, the twisting line of the Grey Corries appears, a tangle of narrow ridges bathed in pale quartzite scree winding away into the middle distance. In the far distance to the right of Aonach Beag, the instantly recognisable distant summit of Schiehallion pokes up on a clear day, appearing as a volcano-like shapely pointed peak piercing up into the sky. Unseen from this distant western vantage point is the long east ridge leading walkers up from Braes of Foss to the summit.

Moving to the rounded southern margin of the plateau, the entire Mamore Range is revealed, each summit unique and offering an alternative exhilarating challenge to the mountain explorer. In the west, smooth grassy ridges rise to the rounded red granite summits of Mullach nan Coirean and Meall a' Chaorainn (**Route 7**), beyond which sparkle the blue waters of Loch Linnhe. Adjacent Stob Ban appears much wilder and rockier, impressive cliffs, crags and buttresses hanging off the tiny pointed pale quartzite summit (**Route 10**). To the east, the immense bulk and fine pointed summit of Binnein Mor contrasts sharply with the lower blunt scree-covered cone of Binnein Beag (**Route 16**). Meanwhile in centre stage rises the impressive bulk of Sgurr a' Mhaim, with its majestic and conspicuous north-facing glacially sculpted corrie, Coire Sgorach. The quartzite and schistose summits of An Gearanach, Stob Coire a' Chairn, Am Bodach and Sgurr an Iubhair encircle Coire a' Mhail, and collectively with Sgurr a' Mhaim comprise the Ring of Steall (**Route 15**).

Beyond the Mamores, the fragile pinnacled ridge of the Aonach Eagach rises amongst a sea of other peaks, the most distinguishable being Bidean nam Bian, often holding snow well into summer in secluded north-facing corries, and the summits of Buachaille Etive Mor at the head of Rannoch Moor. A whole tangle of peaks spread out to the west and north, tailing away to the North Atlantic Ocean, with the rugged pointed pinnacles of the Black Cuillin on Skye visible on a clear day.

Return via the outbound route back to the Glen Nevis Visitor Centre, taking an average of about 3 hours from the summit. Even though the recently constructed tower-like cairns highlight the route, a compass is still an essential tool to safely navigate off the summit plateau during thick fog or snow cover. Furthermore, some walkers unfortunately build cairns haphazardly across the summit plateau in celebration of their ascent, so navigating using the positions of cairns may be misleading. From the trig point walk 150m on a grid bearing of 231° to avoid Gardyloo Gulley, then continue to walk on a grid bearing of 282°, to safely clear the summit plateau and steer clear of the mountain's North Face and then Five Finger Gulley (remembering to allow for magnetic variations over time).

The descent down the western face of the Ben and then the southern and western slopes of Meall an t-Suidhe to Glen Nevis is long, arduous and especially hard on the knees. The screes down the western face of the Ben can be slippery underfoot during the descent, whilst the fine gravelly dust that becomes menacingly attached to your walking boots acts as a wonderful lubricant, facilitating a slide down the smooth granite blocks on the path down Meall an t-Suidhe. Therefore descend slowly and aim for granite blocks with an irregular top surface to place weight upon. Many walkers probably wish they had the supple legs of a sheep or deer during this descent, allowing them to effortlessly bounce down the steep slopes into the darkening glen below.

Sgurr a' Mhaim and Stob Ban above a misty Glen Nevis from the
Ben Nevis Mountain Track in late autumn

The busy summit plateau of Ben Nevis with its trig point, emergency
shelter and observatory ruins, from the head of Gardyloo Gulley

Route 10:

The Stob Ban and Mullach nan Coirean Circuit

This fine circuit links the two contrasting Munros lying at the western end of the impressive Mamore Ridgeline, encircling the attractive rugged head of Coire Dheirg. This is the easiest of the circular routes in the Mamores described in this book and provides plenty of geological interest. Whilst the sharp pointed crags, buttresses and cliffs of Stob Ban are composed of bright white quartzite, the rounded grassy ridges and crags of Mullach nan Coirean have been carved out of attractive red granite, intruded into the prevailing metamorphic Dalradian bedrock at the end of the Caledonian Orogeny.

These attractive summits are linked by fine ridges, all part of the east-west trending Mamore Ridgeline. The east ridge of Stob Ban becomes steep, rocky and exposed towards the top with some scrambling, whilst the ridge to Mullach nan Coirean involves mostly easy walking with a short section of optional scrambling through the middle section.

Typical of all Munro summits in the Mamores, the views from the summits are awe-inspiring, especially across the lochs and peaks towards the west coast, as well as east to the Devil's Ridge and the impressive bulks of the central-eastern Mamores. This circuit could be walked in either direction, although for the less experienced, an ascent of Stob Ban's east ridge is probably easier than a steep descent on scree. Along with the Ring of Steall, this is one of the most popular circuits in the Mamores; however this popularity is dwarfed into insignificance when compared to the likes of Ben Nevis, so it is quite easy to have the fantastic views from the summits of these two Munros to yourself.

The Stob Ban and Mullach nan Coirean Circuit	
Difficulty	Medium
Distance	13.4 km (8.3 miles)
Cumulative ascent	1,160m
Approximate time taken	6-8 hours
Munros	Stob Ban (999m) Mullach nan Coirean (939m)
Subsidiary Tops	Mullach nan Coirean SE Top (917m)
Advisories	• Good level of fitness required • Specialist equipment and experience required when under snow/ice • Several short sections of optional scrambling • A couple of steep ascents and descents on scree

Route 10 Summary

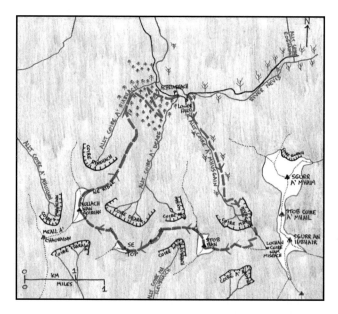

Route 10
Sketch Map

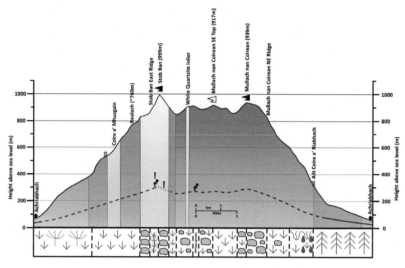

Route 10 Walk Profile

Achriabhach to Coire a' Mhusgain

The route starts at a small path across a stile just north of the Lower Falls car park and immediately south of the main Lower Falls waterfall in Glen Nevis. The car can either be parked at Lower Falls car park (where a fee is charged), at a parking space just north of the Lower Falls waterfall, or at the smaller car park at Achriabhach about 300m to the west, where the walk will end.

The small path temporarily becomes a wider track as it climbs towards the increasingly tight confines of Coire a' Mhusgain, but soon becomes much rougher as it ascends progressively higher above the grassy meadows of lower Glen Nevis. Ignore any paths branching off to the left towards Sgurr a' Mhaim, and instead follow the rough path ascending roughly parallel with the Allt Coire a' Mhusgain over blocks and rubble of schist and granite.

Up ahead the path enters Coire a' Mhusgain and contours high above the Allt Coire a' Mhusgain, clinging to the steep grassy south-

152

western slopes of Sgurr a' Mhaim. The middle section of Coire a' Mhusgain is a delight, another hanging glacially-scoured U-shaped valley, which about 13,000 years ago supported a small mountain glacier. This small glacier would have carved its way down to a large valley glacier filling the bulk of Glen Nevis, much like the confluence between the Allt Coire a' Mhusgain and the River Nevis. The erosion and transport of fine rock flour downslope by the slow erosive action of the glaciers resulted in deposition of a fairly thick glaciogenic sediment sequence across Glen Nevis, creating the fertile glen that we know today.

Crooked and stunted silver birch trees attractively cling to the steep grassy western slopes of Sgurr a' Mhaim, whose immense bulk fills the view to the east. These slopes plunge into a narrow gorge, through which the Allt Coire a' Mhusgain tumbles in a series of cascades and waterfalls. Meanwhile across the western side, the impossibly steep and grassy eastern slopes of Stob Ban's north ridge close in, conjuring a distinct sense of claustrophobia.

As progress is made up the valley, the tiny pointed twin summits of Stob Ban rise majestically high above to the SW, the southernmost being the higher. Impressive quartzite crags support the summit and hang precariously off its eastern face, steep screes cascading down the intervening gullies and crevasses which hold snow well into spring. The watershed at the head of Coire a' Mhusgain rises up to the south, comprising a high bealach between the lofty summits of Stob Ban and Sgurr an Iubhair. To the SE, the pinnacled crest of the Devil's Ridge runs parallel yet high above, forming a northern spur connecting the bulk of Sgurr a' Mhaim to the rounded summit of Sgurr an Iubhair on the main spine of the Mamore Ridgeline.

After just over 2km of walking up the valley you will reach a junction, where you should take the better defined path which hairpins off to the left. This rubbly path then starts to climb higher up the steep grassy western face of the Devil's Ridge via a series of tight zigzags, before running roughly parallel to the Allt Coire a' Mhusgain once more somewhat higher up. The right option at the junction continues to run roughly parallel with the river, then terminates at sheer impassable cliffs along the Allt Coire a' Mhusgain itself. This may represent the former path up the valley before it was obliterated by the ongoing erosive action of wind and water, which all too frequently batter this wild mountainous terrain.

Several tributaries draining the steep slopes of Sgurr a' Mhaim and the Devil's Ridge must be forded, some of which form impressive waterfalls as they cascade down the steep slope in a series of terraces. Ferns and mosses are abundant in the damp, shady and sheltered ravines at the base of these falls. Water bottles should be filled here, as once the bealach below Stob Ban is attained, no more water will be available until the descent off Mullach nan Coirean at the end of the day.

The valley sides become increasingly steep and close in towards the rugged head of Coire a' Mhusgain, as roaring waterfalls along the Allt Coire a' Mhusgain become ever more frequent and impressive. The path progressively climbs to the head of the corrie, full of wild, untamed and undulating topography, the site of the former head of the mountain glacier about 13,000 years ago. The rough path then climbs in a couple of wide zigzags out of the corrie across grassy terrain to a small cairn at the high bealach between Sgurr an Iubhair and Stob Ban at about 760m altitude. The craggy east face of Stob Ban towers high above to the west, a complex tangle of pale quartzite crags, buttresses and scree shoots commanding an air of superiority over your lowly position, still greater than 200m beneath the summit of the mountain.

There is a fine view northwards along the line of lower Glen Nevis, occupied by grassy meadows and deciduous and coniferous forest, to the right of which vast steep slopes soar to the rounded summits of Meall an t-Suidhe and Ben Nevis.

To the south, the well-walked and well-built track of the West

Highland Way runs almost as straight as a Roman road along the northern bank of the Allt Nathrach towards Kinlochleven and the long and narrow body of Loch Leven, whilst the Devil's Ridge and Sgurr a' Mhaim form impressive features to the NE. An easy detour can be made eastward along a small dirt path hewn into the grassy slopes on the northern side of the bealach to the attractive Lochan Coire nam Miseach, a roughly circular loch filling a depression below the quartzite screes and cliffs of Sgurr an Iubhair. Blocks of schist and quartzite glisten beneath the crystal clear waters, whilst the abundance of green waterweed in the centre gives the loch a greenish appearance when viewed from above.

The East Ridge of Stob Ban
to the summit (999m)

From the bealach, follow the grassy slopes westward towards the base of Stob Ban's east ridge. A very steep grassy section must be climbed first, beyond which the gradient slackens and the bedrock changes from grey schist to attractive creamy white quartzite, comprising the bulk of Stob Ban. The east ridge then steepens, narrows and becomes very rocky. Steep boulder-strewn slopes lie to the left (south) whilst the ridge falls away in a series of precipitous cliffs and crags to the right (north) into the heart of Coire a' Mhusgain. Therefore it is important to not stray to the north of the ridge crest. The crest of the ridge involves some sections of relatively easy but exposed scrambling, especially higher up beneath the summit. Alternatively, loose slippery scree paths can be traversed, which wind around and across large angular boulders and smoothed slabs of quartzite along the southern margin of the ridge, avoiding the worst of the exposure. Many of the angular quartzite boulders are sharp and a fall on these would certainly cause some discomfort. The steep and rocky east ridge abruptly terminates at the southern margin of the rounded summit, with a short walk northward to the cairn at the top of Stob Ban (999m). The western and southern slopes of the mountain are more rounded, whilst the summit cairn abuts precipitous cliffs and crags guarding the eastern face, analogous to the Aonachs in the eastern Nevis Range. The summit area consists of boggy and grassy terrain, with scattered quartzite boulders dotted over the area and clustered around the summit cairn and eastern slopes.

The summit offers fine views eastward down the tortuous quartzite crest of the mountain's east ridge to the grey western cliffs and screes of Sgurr an Iubhair, beneath which is perched the small and roughly circular Lochan Coire nam Miseach, nestling into the grassy contours high above the head of Coire a' Mhusgain. The jagged grassy crest of the Devil's Ridge protrudes painfully north to the scree-covered summit of Sgurr a' Mhaim, beyond which the high summits of the central-eastern Mamores soar up, the pointed summits of Binnein Mor, Na Gruagaichean and Am Bodach looking particularly impressive. To the north-east, the stupendously steep southern slopes of Ben Nevis rise high above Glen Nevis to the vast summit plateau, beyond which the pointed granite spire of Carn Mor Dearg contrasts with the rounded grassy ridges and summits of Aonach Beag and Aonach Mor.

The Glencoe mountains form a stunning backdrop to the south, leading out eastward to the heathery and boggy wastes of Rannoch Moor, whilst Loch Linnhe shimmers off into the distance beyond the low summits of Mam na Gualainn and Beinn na Caillich. To the west the onward route becomes apparent: initially heading north to descend over Stob Ban's North Top, then following the undulating granite ridge that curves easily around the head of Coire Dheirg, traversing a number of unnamed tops, to reach the grassy slopes and rounded summit of Mullach nan Coirean at its western termination.

The ridge to Mullach nan Coirean (939m)

Descend south from the summit of Stob Ban on a relatively steep gradient across quartzite scree. The angular blocks again have many sharp and pointed surfaces, so care should be taken to not slip up on these. Gullies, crevasses and scree shoots of the mountain's east face cut quite far into the summit ridge in places, so walkers should keep to the western side of the ridge crest during poor visibility or snow cover. By peering carefully down these gullies in clear weather, the route taken earlier in the day up through beautiful Coire a' Mhusgain can be seen, hundreds of metres below.

You will reach the subsidiary lower northern summit of Stob Ban, still on the sharp angular quartzite boulders, the ridge almost reaching a level gradient at this point and projecting towards the NNE. Continue to descend, veering a little to the left (west) towards the base of this second descent to pick up a well-worn small path. This path contours westward along the grassy southern slopes of the ridge to Mullach nan Coirean, before picking up the ridge crest again at a low point once the north ridge of Stob Ban has been bypassed. The bedrock changes here to blocks of red granite, and this reliable igneous rock will be beneath your feet for much of the remainder of the walk.

Climb easily over a pleasant mixture of weathered granite rubble and patchy rough vegetation to a small unnamed Top, composed of the same pale angular quartzite blocks as Stob Ban. This unnamed little white peak represents a small quartzite inlier and stands out clearly from the remainder of the red granite ridge towards Mullach nan Coirean, the white quartzite around the summit cairn taking on the appearance of a cap of residual winter snow persistently clinging to the small exposed summit. From this peak there's a fine profile of the north ridge of Stob Ban, the subsidiary summits descending progressively towards the north. The first two summits are coated in the infamous angular quartzite scree, however the lower summits become increasingly grassy and vegetated, connected by narrow grassy ridges and steeper smooth rock faces. Stob Ban itself appears almost as impressive from the west as from the east. The attractive quartzite buttresses and crags may be absent, but the steep smooth slopes plunge hundreds of metres south and west towards the valley of the Allt Nathrach far below. These slopes are bathed in attractive pale white quartzite, appearing again like a thick coat of snow, especially when illuminated by a ray of sunlight.

The immense scree-covered mass of the Sgurr a' Mhaim Massif fills the view beyond. Lochan Meall an t-Suidhe, nicknamed the "Halfway Lochan", nestles into the high boggy bealach between Meall an t-Suidhe and Ben Nevis, the translucent loch reflecting the colour of the overhead sky. Immediately below, the Allt Coire a' Dheirg crashes in a series of torrents and cascades down towards a confluence with the River Nevis in the tranquil glen far below, before winding away northward then westward towards Loch Linnhe and the North Atlantic.

Continue on westward over the granite ridge, much of the ridge involving easy walking over patchy vegetation and small blocks of intensely weathered granite. The crest becomes narrow and rocky through the middle section with a short spell of optional scrambling, fairly exposed on the northern side, where steep cliffs and granite crags descend down the headwall of Coire Dheirg. Numerous remote lochans are perched in high boggy depressions above the head of Coire Dheirg, with small streams issuing from these water bodies and plunging down steep granite slopes to the infant Allt Coire a' Dheirg far below. A small path on the gentler southern slopes bypasses all of this exposure and provides easy walking. Walking along this ridge also allows fine views to the west, where the blue waters of Loch Linnhe shimmer attractively and are accompanied by a tangle of mountain peaks stretching out to the vagaries of the North Atlantic.

The ridge becomes wider and the terrain increasingly grassy, peaty and boggy as the SE Top of Mullach nan Coirean is reached (917m). A number of small pools here play host to a surprisingly abundant array of aquatic life in summertime, albeit lagging several months behind similar aquatic life forms across the rest of Britain due to the cold high-altitude climate. Following a small descent, the path climbs at a moderate gradient through rubbly granite to the rounded summit of Mullach nan Coirean (939m), with some attractive quartz veins and euhedral crystals preserved in the granite rubble on this ascent.

The rounded granite summit of Mullach nan Coirean offers a fine view westward along the length of Loch Linnhe, along with the complex tangle of peaks approaching the Scottish west coast. There is also an impressive view eastward along the Mamore Ridgeline to the vast pale screes of Stob Ban, Sgurr a' Mhaim and Sgurr an Iubhair, contrasting with the grassy Devil's Ridge connecting the latter two peaks. The high summits of Binnein Mor, Na Gruagaichean and Am Bodach punch up in the background, whilst the massive rounded bulk of the Ben Nevis Massif is dominant across the open void of Glen Nevis.

The descent from Mullach nan Coirean and back to Achriabhach

Head north then north-east across the wide granite summit plateau to descend via Mullach nan Coirean's NE ridge, which forms the NW rim of Coire Dheirg and the high watershed between the Allt Coire a' Dheirg and Allt Coire a' Riabhach. The descent is initially relatively steep over granite boulders and slippery scree along a fairly narrow ridge, guarded to the right (south) by granite cliffs and crags plunging into the head of Coire Dheirg. The ridge widens lower down and becomes increasingly grassy and heathery as the gradient slackens and a deer fence joins from the right (south) side.

At this point, two descent routes become available. The first involves turning to the right (south) and descending very steep heathery and grassy slopes into Coire Dheirg next to the fence, then following a small boggy path through dense forest to reach the main Land Rover track above the car park at Achriabhach. The second option, described here, continues to descend the NE ridge as it swings towards the NNE and is probably the easier option.

A very rough stony path starts to descend the extremely steep heathery and bouldery hillside next to the large fence. Follow the line of the wire fence down to the base of the steep slope, where there is an area of very boggy terrain in a sump at the base of Mullach nan Coirean's NE face. All of the water draining the catchment area between the summit of Mullach nan Coirean and its enclosing N and NE ridges accumulates on this perennially wet slack gradient. Inch your way carefully through the waterlogged ground to reach a large stile crossing the fence followed so far. It is possible to fill water bottles here by descending westward adjacent to the fence to reach the Allt Coire a' Riabhach.

The path on the opposite side of the stile used to lead through a dense coniferous forest plantation; however this has been felled in recent years. The well-made small path now descends the bare slope through a maze of pine stumps and branches, roughly parallel to the Allt Coire a' Riabhach, which crashes through a hidden valley out of sight to the NW. The small path terminates at a wide Land Rover track at the base of this slope. Turn right and follow this track as it descends at an easy gradient via a series of broad zigzags through predominantly thick coniferous forest. Be careful to bear left at the first junction, then sharply right at the second junction, to emerge through a metal gate back to the car park at Achriabhach in lower Glen Nevis. The Lower Falls car park is located about 300m eastward along the road.

Looking into the head of Coire a' Mhusgain in summer

Panorama eastward from Stob Ban

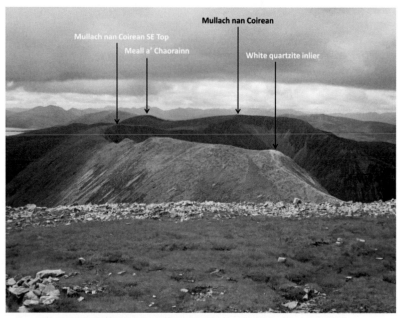

Panorama westward from Stob Ban to Mullach nan Coirean

The Nevis Range from the unnamed white quartzite peak

Stob Ban from the unnamed white quartzite peak in summer

Stob Ban from the unnamed white quartzite peak in winter

Stob Ban and Sgurr a' Mhaim from Mullach nan Coirean's SE Top in summer

Stob Ban and Sgurr a' Mhaim from Mullach nan Coirean's SE Top in winter

164

Thick cornices rim and overhang the northern margin
of the ridge to Mullach nan Coirean

Mullach nan Coirean from its SE Top in winter

Route 11:

Ben Nevis via Coire Leis

This climb allows the walker to experience the best Ben Nevis has to offer and provides a complete experience of the mountain's finest feature, its mighty North Face, without the need for any rock-climbing equipment. The route firstly traverses the rough and remote head of Coire Leis directly beneath the North Face, with an awe-inspiring view of its mighty cliffs, crags and corries from below. Britain's highest mountain is then ascended via a steep boulder field on its south-eastern slopes, with a fantastic opportunity to peer down on that same impressive North Face from above. The upper part of Coire Leis comprises some very wild, rough and rocky terrain where some steep and exposed scree slopes must be ascended; therefore this climb is better suited to more competent hill walkers with experience of such terrain. This route should only be attempted during summer conditions, when winter snow and ice have receded from the headwall of Coire Leis, and then only during calm and settled weather. The risk of falling rock debris from the immense cliffs of Ben Nevis' North Face is likely to increase during very wet or stormy conditions, when crossing the Allt a' Mhuilinn below the CIC Hut may also become more difficult.

Ben Nevis via Coire Leis	
Difficulty	Hard
Distance	15.5 km (9.6 miles)
Cumulative ascent	1,430m
Approximate time taken	6-7 hours
Munros	Ben Nevis (1,344m)
Subsidiary Tops	-
Advisories	• High level of fitness and stamina required • Good height for heights required for traversing the headwall of Coire Leis • Should not be attempted when snow/ice line the headwall of Coire Leis or during stormy weather • Steep ascent over rough terrain and loose scree

Route 11 Summary

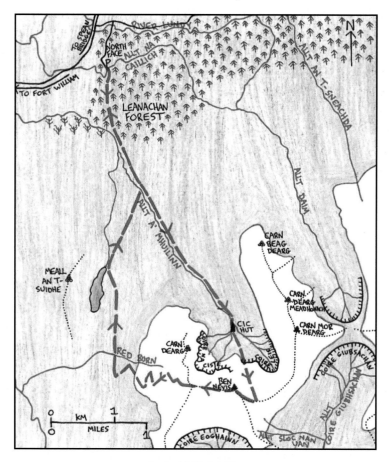

Route 11 Sketch Map

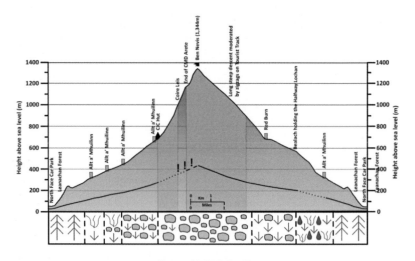

Route 11 Walk Profile

Starting at the North Face car park, take the well-made path through Leanachan Forest involving several stages of quite steep ascent, to enter the hanging valley of the Allt a' Mhuilinn. Cross the stile then follow the path up the valley roughly parallel with the river, along its north-eastern bank, to reach the CIC Hut. The infant Allt a' Mhuilinn must be forded just below the hut via a series of large granite blocks used as stepping stones, which may be difficult when the river is in spate after heavy rainfall.

Continue past the hut into the wild, rough and remote head of Coire Leis. The path becomes increasingly indistinct and difficult to follow, often obliterated by landslides of grey andesite scree derived from the adjacent cliffs of Ben Nevis, which tower high above. Bits and pieces of path can be followed and the walker should aim for the base of Ben Nevis' NE Buttress, the sheer grey cliff that protrudes starkly into the head of Coire Leis straight ahead. The terrain is rough and rocky; with the angular andesite blocks and scree typically loose and liable to moving under the feet.

The head of Coire Leis essentially consists of a vast and

168

increasingly steep boulder field, the traverse of which is very tough going. The best route therefore follows a broken path as it skirts along the edge of this boulder field, hugging the base of the impressive cliffs supporting Ben Nevis' broad summit plateau. Patches of grass and moss have developed here, making for easier walking.

Once Ben Nevis' NE Buttress has been rounded, continue to skirt the boulder field on the broken rough path as it follows the edge of Ben Nevis' solid andesite cliffs and starts to climb quite steeply. The vast boulder field at the head of Coire Leis is predominantly derived from these andesite cliffs; therefore walkers should always be alert to the risk of falling rock debris from high above. The path then slants across a steep rocky slope and a short section of boulders comprising the headwall of Coire Leis, to arrive at the end of the Carn Mor Dearg (CMD) Arête, where it merges with a steep boulder field below the summit plateau of Ben Nevis. This final ascent should not be attempted if the headwall of Coire Leis is coated in snow or ice and a good head for heights is essential, as there are steep drops of more than 100m into the head of Coire Leis below. A large well-built tower-like cairn has been built on this part of the CMD Arête to mark the point where a line of abseil posts used to lead down the headwall of Coire Leis. These were removed during the summer of 2012 as they were old and deemed to be no longer safe to use.

Turn right and climb a steep boulder field to the summit of Ben Nevis on a faint paler-coloured scree path, taking care to not stray to the right of this path as steep cliffs and crags line the eastern margin of this deceptively wide boulder slope. The summit of the Ben is abruptly reached as the slope gradient eases off. On a clear day it is worthwhile taking time to savour the incredible 360° panorama from the summit, moving cautiously over towards the margins of the broad summit plateau for the best views.

The descent involves returning down the "Mountain Track" as

far as Halfway Lochan, including a chance to fill the water bottles at the Red Burn just above the loch. Once down near Halfway Lochan, the Mountain Track turns abruptly left and slants down the steep western slopes of Meall an t-Suidhe, involving a series of zigzags. The route back to the North Face car park heads straight on ahead however, along a well-made path due north and parallel with the Halfway Lochan. When the path splits up ahead, bear left to arrive at the far (northern) end of the loch, where the path fizzles out at a small burn which drains from its foot.

From the northern end of Halfway Lochan, head due north over rough and heathery ground, boggy in places, towards the Allt a' Mhuilinn burn below. There is no clear path for this section of the walk, although bits and pieces of path can be located in places; simply head towards the Allt a' Mhuilinn crashing over rocks in the centre of the valley ahead.

Once down, the river has to be forded. When the level is low, it is often possible to find a place where there are enough stepping stones for the burn to be forded with dry feet, but be cautious of rocks that move when weight is placed on them. If the river level is higher, then a cold icy paddle across a shallower section may be necessary, representing an ideal opportunity to freshen up. It is worth bearing in mind that the river may be completely impassable when in spate after heavy rainfall, and this return route is therefore not advisable under such conditions.

Clamber up the northern bank, and locate a path just to the north, which has descended from high up in Coire Leis. This is the outbound path used earlier in the day; therefore from here return via the outbound route, back north-westward through Leanachan Forest to North Face car park.

Alternatives

If the inevitable crowds on the summit plateau of Ben Nevis are too off-putting, you might turn north-east above the head of Coire Leis and instead of climbing the steep monotonous scree slope to the summit of Britain's highest, negotiate the narrow rocky crest of the CMD Arête to the granite summit of Carn Mor Dearg. Traverse the lower subsidiary summits of the mountain's north ridge, gazing in awe at the spectacular cliffs of Ben Nevis' North Face, then descend the steep and rough western slopes of Carn Beag Dearg to intersect the main path back through Leanachan Forest to the North Face car park.

Looking down the valley of the Allt a' Mhuilinn from the head of Coire Leis

171

Route 12:

The Aonachs

The Aonachs (Aonach Beag and Aonach Mor) represent the two highest points on a vast north-south trending ridge, which also crosses the subsidiary summits of Sgurr a' Bhuic and Stob Coire Bhealaich, forming the high eastern barrier of the Nevis Range. When translated into English, the names of the mountains are somewhat erroneous, with Aonach Mor translating as "Little Ridge" and Aonach Beag as "Big Ridge", despite the fact that the summit of Aonach Beag is 13m higher than Aonach Mor. When viewed from any northern or eastern vantage point in the Spean Valley or Great Glen, it is quite clear that the names refer to the respective mass of the mountains. While Aonach Beag forms a shapely rounded summit, Aonach Mor comprises a long broad summit ridge and a much greater bulk.

A climb of both Munros is a revelation for any walker in the Nevis Range, not least to simply see the huge contrast between the bare summit and impressive crags of Aonach Beag and the tame wide grassy summit ridge of Aonach Mor. These mountains require a little more effort to reach than the others in the range as all the car parks are in the west, however once up on one, it is only a short walk to the other.

Many walkers think the obtrusive machinery of the Nevis Range Ski Centre on the northern slopes of Aonach Mor significantly scar and ruin the wild feel of the mountain, although the Nevis Gondola in summer can be used to ride more than halfway up the northern slopes of Aonach Mor in 12-15 minutes and relieve a significant portion of the climb. The route described here from Glen Nevis takes in the best the mountains have to offer, ascending all the Munro Tops along the ridge from the south, to reach the northern summit of Aonach Mor without once gaining any hint of the existence of a ski and outdoor activity centre sprawling across the mountain's north face.

The Aonachs	
Difficulty	Hard
Distance	16.1 km (9.7 miles)
Cumulative ascent	1,340m
Approximate time taken	7-9 hours
Munros	Aonach Beag (1,234m) Aonach Mor (1,221m)
Subsidiary Tops	Stob Coire Bhealaich (1,101m) Sgurr a' Bhuic (963m)
Advisories	• High level of fitness and stamina required • Unsuitable during high winds and on short mid-winter days • Very steep descent on heavily eroded path and scree off Aonach Mor, which should not be attempted when coated in snow/ice

Route 12 Summary

Route 12 Walk Profile

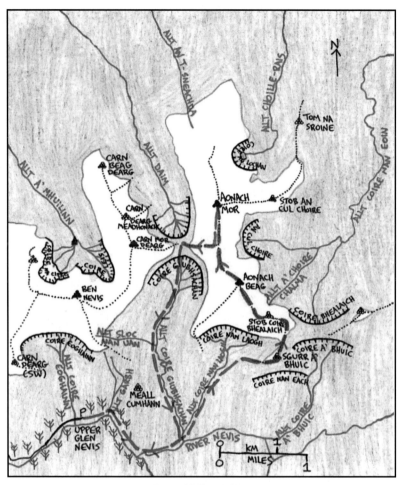

Route 12 Sketch Map

Nevis Gorge to Sgurr a' Bhuic (963m)

From the popular car park at the road end in Glen Nevis, take the path leading eastward through deciduous forest into the narrow Nevis Gorge, before emerging into the attractive grassy Steall Meadows. Follow the occasionally muddy path along the northern bank of the Nevis River, then cross a wooden bridge across the Allt Coire Giubhsachan to reach the Steall Ruins.

The main path through Glen Nevis should be vacated at the Steall Ruins and it is here that the ascent begins. Looking to the N/NE, the Allt Coire nan Laogh descends steeply from high up in Coire nan Laogh, a rugged corrie perched beneath the steep grassy southern slopes of Aonach Beag. The Allt Coire nan Laogh flows into the Allt Coire Giubhsachan just upstream from the bridge, which in turn is a major tributary to the River Nevis just downstream.

Head north-eastward from the Steall Ruins on a small path that starts to climb the slopes to the right (east) of the Allt Coire nan Laogh, and roughly parallel with the river. The small path is composed of rubbly schist and quartzite blocks, as height is soon gained above the valley floor in Glen Nevis. The Allt Coire nan Laogh, close on the left, tumbles and cascades alongside in a series of foaming waterfalls. This river represents the final chance to fill up with water for some time, the next opportunities being during the descent off Aonach Mor or through Coire Giubhsachan, so it is advisable to fill up with water here, where the path passes close to the river.

The path climbs roughly parallel to the river for some distance, then starts to climb high above it and becomes increasingly indistinct across the grassy western slopes of Sgurr a' Bhuic. From this point, the best method of ascent is to contour round to the northern side of Sgurr a' Bhuic's western Top, and then progressively head up onto the wide blocky crest of the summit ridge. The crest of this wide and increasingly rubbly and scree-covered quartzite ridge rises at a moderate gradient eastward to the small quartzite cairn at the summit of Sgurr a' Bhuic (963m), the southernmost peak on the N-S oriented Aonach Ridge. The summit cairn abuts a precipitous drop to the east, towards the boggy col with Sgurr Choinnich Beag, so it is important to never stray onto scree or snow cornices east of the cairn.

The pointed summit of Sgurr a' Bhuic is perhaps the best viewpoint for the western Grey Corries and central-eastern Mamores, lying close at hand to the east and south of the summit cairn respectively. To the east, a fine grassy asymmetrical ridge winds away eastward from a boggy bealach at the head of Coire a' Bhuic, across the subsidiary bump of Sgurr Choinnich Beag to the pointed summit of Sgurr Choinnich Mor. The scree-covered western slopes and pointed summits of Stob Coire Easain and Stob Coire an Laoigh poke out on the twisting Grey Corries ridgeline, beyond Sgurr Choinnich Mor. The River Nevis meanders away through a wide open valley between the Grey Corries and the eastern Mamores towards Rannoch Moor. To the south, the superb E-W oriented Mamore Range stretches out across the southern margin of Glen Nevis in all its glory, with only the quartzite summit of Stob Ban missing from the scene, obscured behind the bulk of Sgurr a' Mhaim. Sgurr a' Bhuic is already 20 metres higher than the blunt cone of Binnein Beag, with the rounded summit of Sgurr Eilde Mor contrasting starkly with the pointed summits and ridges of Binnein Mor, whilst the large Lochan Coire an Lochain fills the boggy bealach between the two summits.

The An Gearanach-An Garbhanach and Devil's Ridge-Sgurr a' Mhaim spurs protrude northward from the main east-west oriented Mamore Ridgeline, comprising Na Gruagaichean, Stob Coire a' Chairn, Am Bodach and Sgurr an Iubhair. Steep grassy and rocky northern slopes plunge abruptly into the gash occupied today by the River Nevis. Looking due south, there's a fine view up the grassy course of the Allt Coire na Gabhalach into the remote heads of Coire

Gabhail and Coire an Easain. The sprawling red grassy ridges and rounded granite summit of Mullach nan Coirean complete the western end of the Mamore Ridgeline, much gentler in appearance. To the NW, the vast grey andesite screes and crags of Ben Nevis' southern slopes poke up behind the grassy SW ridge of Aonach Beag, with the delicate line of the CMD Arête curving up to merge with a steep boulder field beneath the summit.

Looking to the north, the onward route over Stob Coire Bhealaich to Aonach Beag can be seen along an asymmetrical ridge crest. The steep, grassy western slopes plunge into Coire nan Laogh, whilst a sheer impenetrable striated grey wall of solid schist and scree abuts the ridge crest to the east. This is the start of the Aonach Ridge, with a similar precipitous east face continuing some 4km (2.5 miles) to the north, impressively holding snow in narrow gullies and crevasses throughout much of the summer.

On to Stob Coire Bhealaich (1101m) and Aonach Beag (1234m)

Descend relatively steeply northwards from Sgurr a' Bhuic, taking care over the often slippery scree. It is wise to keep to the western side of the ridge crest, to avoid a dangerous slip close to the precipitous eastern face. A faint scree path runs along the crest of the ridge down to the col between Sgurr a' Bhuic and Stob Coire Bhealaich, above Coire nan Laogh. Continue along the ridge, close to the eastern face, as it starts to climb northwards towards Stob Coire Bhealaich over large boulders. Soon it is possible to pick up an easily discernible small path rising north along the ridge as it becomes grassy higher up. The crest of the ridgeline then turns abruptly to the west and becomes increasingly narrow and rocky, with cliffs and crags guarding the northern margin of the ridge. The path keeps to the steep but less precipitous grassy southern slopes as the small rocky Munro Top of Stob Coire Bhealaich (1101m) is traversed.

By now the craggy east face of Aonach Beag comes into view, large wedges of snow nestling suspended in gullies and crevasses. Beyond, the long ridge of Aonach Mor stretches out with numerous ridges radiating off and down its eastern face, intervening remote corries again providing a summer refuge for the remnant and constantly receding winter snows. Aonach Beag appears the far wilder and more untameable beast from this aspect, and this notion is confirmed once the two summits are traversed. Sgurr a' Bhuic now lies beneath to the south, a rocky ridge progressively rising to the pointed summit then dropping precipitously down its eastern face, all bathed in attractive white quartzite scree and taking on the appearance of a fluorescent pyramid.

Continue on the small path along the rocky ridge westwards until the ridge swings to the NW, takes in a small descent, becomes grassy and widens. Gullies of the eastern face start to cut into the ridge, with suspended snow wedges, the remnant winter cornices, close at hand on the right (east). Far beneath, a complex network of small burns cut a rocky tortuous course from the head of Coire Bhealaich over undulating topography, fed by meltwater from the winter snows still held in the cold eastern face. Descend a little, then climb up the final moderately steep grassy slopes with patchy scree to the rounded summit of Aonach Beag. At the start of this ascent, a path swings off to the left (west) across the grassy southern slopes of Aonach Beag. This should be ignored and the smaller path adjacent and parallel to the precipitous eastern face should be followed.

The peculiar broad rounded summit of Aonach Beag (1234m) suddenly appears as the slope gradient eases off, covered in scattered platy blocks of schist wedged in smoothed and striated but firm mossy mud. The summit itself is almost devoid of any other vegetation, but banks of moss and grass coalesce beneath the muddy summit plateau and along the rim of its eastern face. The summit area is snow-covered for many months of the year, but frequently battered by the prevailing cold and wet south-westerly winds during the few months of exposure, as the winter snows temporarily recede. The muddy convex western and southern slopes curve away initially gently from the summit, however the summit cairn, as on Sgurr a' Bhuic, abuts the precipitous eastern face of the Aonach Ridge. Therefore walkers should not venture east of the summit cairn.

The summit of Aonach Beag is a fine vantage point for the entire Nevis Range, as Ben Nevis and Carn Mor Dearg rise up starkly across the opposite side of Coire Giubhsachan, whilst the flat-topped Aonach Mor looms up to the north. The pyramidal summit of Carn Mor Dearg takes centre stage, from which radiate three ridges. The curving east ridge reaches out towards you across Coire Giubhsachan, whilst the CMD Arête twists round to connect with Ben Nevis, it's precipitous grassy and rocky south-eastern walls rising abruptly across the glen. The fine north ridge connects to Carn Dearg Meadhonach, whose pinnacled east ridge makes an imposing feature against an impressive backdrop of the NW Highlands. The grey andesite cliffs and crags of Ben Nevis' North Face soar up above the line of the CMD Arête.

To the north, the wide grassy ridge of Aonach Mor progressively rises towards the summit, with a distinctive brown dirt path threading its way up the easy slope. Even from here, the contrast between the tops of the two Munros can be easily appreciated. The best views to the west and north are actually from the margins of the broad rounded summit plateau. The Mamores and Grey Corries also look fine from the summit, but rather more distant than from Sgurr a' Bhuic earlier in the day. Peering carefully over the eastern face reveals a complex series of crags and buttresses supporting the summit plateau, descending abruptly into the remote rugged head of Coire Bhealaich far below.

On to Aonach Mor (1221m)

Head north across the muddy summit plateau, admiring the thick striated and grooved wedges of dirty-looking snow clinging to the cold and rocky eastern face of the mountain. Pick up a small rocky path descending towards the bealach with Aonach Mor, close to cliffs of the eastern face. The ridge leading down northward from Aonach Beag is also convex in nature, starting initially at a gentle gradient but becoming increasingly steep and craggy just above the grassy bealach. Keeping to the eroded path involves little difficulty during the summer months, though care should be taken on the steep craggy section just above the bealach, where the scree is rather loose and slippery.

The climb up onto Aonach Mor is the easiest of the day, up a fairly gentle gradient on a dirt path along the wide grassy crest of the Aonach Ridge. The large summit cairn on Aonach Mor sits in the middle of the relatively wide grassy ridge, in complete contrast to the previous summits. The ridge as a whole also appears far tamer than much of the walk so far, with the extensive grass cover and gently climbing dirt path being more akin to a walk up a hill in southern England, rather than the final climb up a 4000-footer. The mountain consequently does not have the same wild feel as the others in the range.

A short walk to the edges of the wide ridge allow for fine views to the west and east. The attractive red summits along Carn Mor Dearg's north ridge dominate the view to the west, rising southward from the rounded summit of Carn Beag Dearg, over an unnamed top to the pointed summit of Carn Dearg Meadhonach, then up to the pyramidal summit of Carn Mor Dearg. Aprons of pink granite scree partially blanket the steep slopes, whilst banks of firm winter snow remain lodged in high rocky granite corries beneath the summits of Carn Mor Dearg and Carn Dearg Meadhonach into early

July. Three ridges radiate eastward off Carn Mor Dearg's north ridge towards the valley of the Allt Daim: the curving east ridge of Carn Mor Dearg, the pinnacled and craggy east ridge of Carn Dearg Meadhonach, and a smooth ridge leading to the unnamed top south of Carn Beag Dearg. Each of these ridges offers a route to the crest of Carn Mor Dearg's north ridge from the east, with varying degrees of difficulty. The dark grey North Face of Ben Nevis looms up above and beyond the twisting line of the CMD Arête, holding vast slopes of inaccessible snow, whilst the Ben's NW Top Carn Dearg appears through the high col between Carn Mor Dearg and Carn Dearg Meadhonach. The view to the east is more open, over the neighbouring scree-covered Munro Top of Stob an Cul Choire to the grey twisting Grey Corrie ridgeline, and into the open partially-forested Spean Valley. A number of small lochans, drained by meandering burns, nestle into the high remote corries of Aonach Mor's eastern face. Banks of snow persist in these corries until early July and are visible from some distance east of Roy Bridge, when travelling westward on the A86.

There are two options for the descent route off Aonach Mor to return to Glen Nevis. These involve either retracing the long outbound route back across Aonach Beag, Stob Coire Bhealaich and Sgurr a' Bhuic, or descending a steep rough spur westward to the bealach with Carn Mor Dearg (Bealach Giubhsachan), followed by a descent through scenic Coire Giubhsachan. The latter option is described below, but whilst being the more interesting route, involves an extremely steep descent off the mountain on slippery scree, and is best attempted by seasoned hill walkers with experience of such terrain. For those with available transport, by far the easiest and quickest descent route is to continue northward and descend the northern face of Aonach Mor, either by foot or by gondola, thereby using the development of the Nevis Range Ski Centre to your advantage.

Descending from Aonach Mor (1221m) to Bealach Giubhsachan (830m) and back to Glen Nevis

Retrace your steps from the summit cairn on the path along the centre of the summit ridge, however about a third of the way down, veer off gently to the right (west) towards the western rim on a faint path, taking care not to venture too close when it is snow covered or in poor visibility. This faint grassy path runs roughly parallel to the western rim, then starts to descend gently along it until reaching a small granite cairn. This cairn marks the descent point from Aonach Mor down a steep and rough spur to Bealach Giubhsachan, but can be difficult to locate in poor visibility. The important fact to remember is that this spur forms the first and steepest rise north of the bealach between Aonach Beag and Aonach Mor. The eroded path down the spur consists of rubble and scree, annoyingly slippery underfoot as the gradient becomes very steep, with the bealach almost directly beneath you far below. Extreme caution should be exercised on this part of the walk. The granite bulk of Carn Mor Dearg now fills your view straight ahead, with the attractive east ridge curving up from Bealach Giubhsachan to the tiny pointed summit, initially wide but becoming increasingly narrow in the upper section. Lower down this steep descent, the path descends adjacent to a small spring issuing from within the bulk of Aonach Mor, and it is possible to fill up with water here.

Finally the boggy Bealach Giubhsachan beneath Carn Mor Dearg is reached, complete with lush green grass, a few small pools and a crumbling granite wall starting up the lower slopes of Carn Mor Dearg's east ridge. Heading to the south across the bealach offers a fine view down much of the length of Coire Giubhsachan, with the Allt Coire Giubhsachan meandering serenely on a gentle boggy gradient in the lower reaches. To the north lies the tighter remote valley of the Allt Daim, between the north ridge of Carn Mor Dearg and Aonach Mor, with the Allt Daim following a rocky course NNW towards the open valley of the Great Glen.

Descend south into the head of Coire Giubhsachan, to locate a small path which develops and runs parallel to the Allt Coire Giubhsachan on the right (west) bank, once it emerges as a spring from within the hillside just beneath the boggy bealach. The path descends initially steeply adjacent to the small stream in steps hewn out of peat and granite sand. Lower down, the path crosses several small streams draining the steep south-eastern walls of the CMD Arête, always keeping fairly close to and on the right bank of the Allt Coire Giubhsachan.

The river begins to attractively meander across the boggy terrain as the gradient slackens towards the outer reaches of Coire Giubhsachan, and the path traverses away from the river for a short distance before reuniting with the river at the entrance to the corrie. This is a fine spot for a bathe in the icy cold waters, as quartz, feldspar and mica, derived from the prevailing granite bedrock upstream, twinkle like semi-precious jewels beneath the crystal clear waters.

From here descend via the fairly steep small stony path on the right (west) bank of the river, often waterlogged after heavy rainfall, down to Glen Nevis, and from there follow the outbound route back through Steall Meadows and the Nevis Gorge to the car park at the road end.

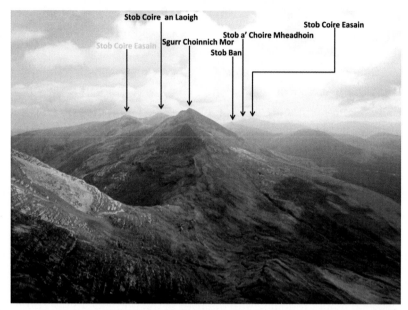

Panorama eastward from Sgurr a' Bhuic

Panorama southward over Sgurr a' Bhuic to the Mamores from Stob Coire Bhealaich

The eastern faces of Aonach Beag and Aonach Mor from Stob Coire Bhealaich

Carn Mor Dearg and Ben Nevis from Aonach Beag

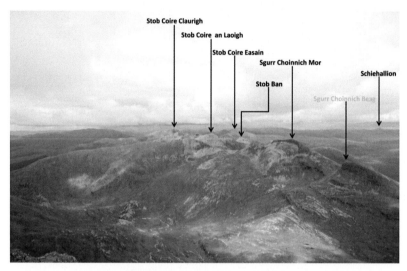

The Grey Corries from Aonach Beag

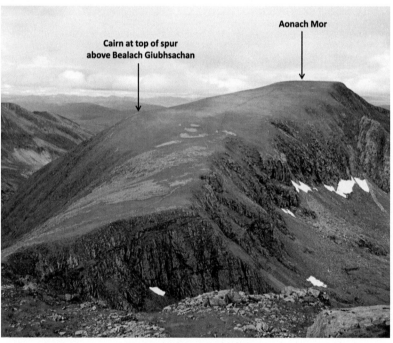

Aonach Mor from Aonach Beag

Carn Mor Dearg and Ben Nevis from Aonach Mor

Rescue helicopter above the summit plateau of Ben Nevis,
with Carn Mor Dearg in the foreground

Route 13:

Ben Nevis and Carn Mor Dearg via the CMD Arête

This is perhaps the "classic" walk in the Nevis Range – if there was one circular walk that must be done by any competent Munro walker to experience the best the Nevis Range has to offer in one day, this is it. This route is a fantastic circuit, linking the contrasting highest and ninth highest mountains in the country via the spectacular Carn Mor Dearg (CMD) Arête. It lies in a wonderfully exposed scenic location and never drops beneath the 1050m contour during over a kilometre of high-altitude ridge-walking perfection.

The traverse of the CMD Arête is understandably quite popular in high summer with perhaps as many as 11 or 12 fellow scramblers on the ridge at the same time, dwarfed into insignificance by the number of "walkers" encountered once the summit plateau of Ben Nevis is reached. A settled, calm and clear day is essential for this one, to experience the Ben's North Face at its best and of course to enjoy the spectacular 360° panorama from the summit of Ben Nevis itself. Indeed this route is inadvisable and potentially dangerous during high winds and requires a completely different set of skills, equipment and experience under the snow and ice of winter.

Many guidebooks on the area suggest walking this route from the Glen Nevis Visitor Centre; however I recommend climbing from the smaller North Face car park near Torlundy (NE of Fort William). This route is becoming increasingly popular with walkers and importantly avoids an unnecessary descent into the glen of the Allt a' Mhuilinn from the bealach containing Lochan Meall an t-Suidhe, therefore making for a slightly easier day.

Ben Nevis and Carn Mor Dearg via the CMD Arête	
Difficulty	Hard
Distance	16.7 km (10.4 miles)
Cumulative ascent	1,500m
Approximate time taken	7-10 hours
Munros	Ben Nevis (1,344m) Carn Mor Dearg (1,220m)
Subsidiary Tops	Carn Dearg Meadhonach (1,179m)
Advisories	• High level of fitness and stamina required • Good head for heights essential • Unsuitable during high winds and on short mid-winter days • The Allt a' Mhuilinn may be impassable if in spate after heavy rainfall • Only to be attempted by those with specialist equipment and experience when under snow/ice • Fairly easy but exposed scrambling along the CMD Arête, but can be partially circumvented • Steep boulderfield ascent onto Ben Nevis

Route 13 Summary

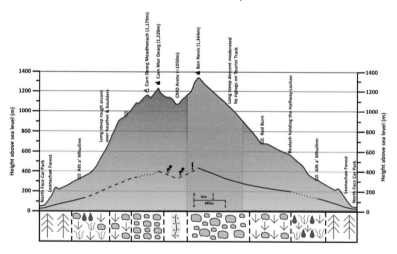

Route 13 Walk Profile

189

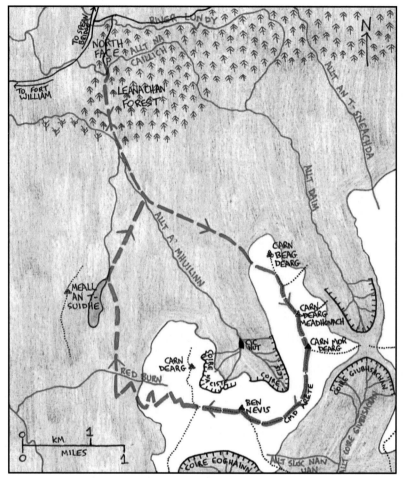

Route 13 Sketch Map

Ascending Carn Mor Dearg
from the North Face car park

Leave the southern end of the North Face car park and take the well-made signposted path through Leanachan Forest to the start of the hanging valley of the Allt a' Mhuilinn. Continue SE into the glen of the Allt a' Mhuilinn, where the path continues on up alongside the river to the CIC Hut before fizzling out in the tight confines of wild upper Coire Leis.

The path therefore needs to be vacated at some point to make the steep climb up onto Carn Mor Dearg's north ridge. Whichever route you choose, the way will be relentlessly steep. Some guidebooks suggest continuing up the valley and ascending the extremely steep heathery and bouldery slopes directly to the summit of Carn Dearg Meadhonach or the bealach north of Carn Mor Dearg, therefore bypassing the top of Carn Beag Dearg. However I would recommend leaving the main path earlier and ascending the western slopes of Carn Beag Dearg via a rough stalker's path. Although the climb is slightly longer than a direct ascent of Carn Dearg Meadhonach, the gradient is not as steep. Having said that, it's still a long slog, and if sunny, it's very easy to get sunburn climbing south-eastward into the morning sun all the way up.

The climb is rough over heather, grass and scattered granite boulders, boggy on the lower slopes, with the rough stalker's path fizzling out in places. This rough path contours to the SW (right) of Carn Beag Dearg, with fantastic views across Coire Leis to the North Face of Ben Nevis throughout. The summit of Carn Beag Dearg can be attained if desired, however it's surrounded by large granite blocks, many of them upturned and some of them movable, though this probably requires more effort than it's worth.

The best route involves heading directly up to the relatively wide crest of Carn Mor Dearg's north ridge just beyond (to the south) of Carn Beag Dearg, where a prominent marked gulley in the hillside can be followed. This gash in the solid granite ridge maintains residual winter snow and ice fairly long into the summer months, carved by a small stream that emerges as a spring from beneath a pile of granite blocks higher up. This is an ideal place to fill up the bottles with crystal clear ice cold water derived from granite bedrock in the heart of Carn Beag Dearg, as there will be no more water throughout the rest of the high ridge walk until the Red Burn is forded, halfway down Ben Nevis on the Mountain Track.

Follow the line of the small stream valley uphill, then continue ESE once this disappears underground to gain the wide ridge crest, where the vast gullied and grassy western wall of Aonach Mor suddenly pops into view. The eastern face of Carn Mor Dearg's north ridge drops away much more steeply than its western face, via a series of steep scree slopes and granite crags to the bleak and little-frequented valley of the Allt Daim far below. Large snow cornices build up along the rim of this eastern face and often overhang it during winter and spring, and it is important to stay on the western side of the ridgeline under these conditions.

The impressive North Face of Ben Nevis fills the view to the west, now running almost parallel with you, all of the corries displayed in their full splendour. Coire na Ciste in particular is a wonderfully complex tangle of rock, snow and water, all coming together temporarily on a sub-horizontal gradient before pouring over the lip of the corrie and plunging hundreds of metres to the rocky valley floor. Tower Ridge rises majestically up from the Douglas Boulder in Coire Leis, and on a fine day it is a common sight to see rock and ice climbers, complete with ropes, helmets and axes, inching their way carefully and painstakingly up the rugged crest.

Impressive banks of muddy snow often still cling to the eastern face of the ridgeline until July; these only become larger and more extensive heading south towards Carn Mor Dearg. Continue SSE along the wide crest of the ridge, which involves easy walking over small blocks of rubbly granite. An unnamed top is reached next, beyond which is a short climb to the summit cairn on Carn Dearg Meadhonach (1179m).

The impressive feature of Carn Dearg Meadhonach is its jagged east ridge, which falls away from the summit in a series of pinnacles guarded by crumbling granite crags and aprons of scree. This could represent an exciting alternative ridge route to the summit of Carn Dearg Meadhonach from the valley of the Allt Daim for an appropriately-attired rock climber, but it is beyond the scope of this book. The east ridge of Carn Mor Dearg is a much easier option when arriving from the east. From the summit of Carn Dearg Meadhonach, the view starts to open up to the south with Carn Mor Dearg taking centre stage and appearing in full view for the first time whilst walking along its north ridge. The pointed pyramidal peak rises impressively straight ahead, vast snow slopes often suspended in a spacious NE-facing corrie enclosed by the ridge to Carn Dearg Meadhonach, the summit of Carn Mor Dearg, and its east ridge. Beyond, the twisting rocky crest of the CMD Arête pokes into view, whilst the vast bulks of Aonach Mor and Aonach Beag stand bold to the east. The distant pointed peak of Schiehallion pokes through the high bealach between these two Munros on a clear day.

Descend from Carn Dearg Meadhonach on a relatively easy gradient to a rocky low section, beneath a final moderately steep climb over granite blocks and rubble to the summit of Carn Mor Dearg, keeping to the relatively wide crest for fine views to the east and west. Attractive euhedral clear quartz crystals are abundant in the granite rubble between Carn Dearg Meadhonach and Carn Mor Dearg, with small samples well worth taking home as a souvenir of the walk.

In clear weather, the summit of Carn Mor Dearg is perhaps the finest vantage point for the magnificent North Face of Ben Nevis. Sheer cliffs 600 metres high, the tallest in Britain, tower high above the remote rugged hanging valley of Coire Leis and tiny CIC hut, the latter appearing as a small dot far below. Vast snow slopes abound in crevasses and hang suspended in remote intricately scoured corries accessible only to the rock and ice climber, more comparable to the eastern face of Aonach Beag than of Aonach Mor, but at an unprecedented scale. Meltwater streams form impressive foaming waterfalls, crashing over vertical cliffs of andesite and recharging remote suspended lochans which are frozen solid in time during the cold winter months. The ant-like figures of countless proud walkers can often be seen (and sometimes heard) swarming across the summit plateau, delighted at having successfully made the trudge up the "Mountain Track" from Achintee, but never able to fully appreciate the grandeur of the mountain's North Face that you see before your eyes.

To the south is the first proper view of the entire length of the CMD Arête from above. The delicate line curves symmetrically and gracefully around the head of Coire Leis to merge with a vast grey boulder field beneath the summit of the UK's highest mountain, with an unequalled backdrop of the Mamores (except for Mullach nan Coirean, hidden behind the bulk of Ben Nevis), then the Glencoe mountains and the northern Blackmount sprawling out towards the horizon, as far as the eye can see. From this superior elevation, you look down on them all.

To the east, the first sign of weakness in the Aonach Mor-Aonach Beag ridge is appreciated, as the twisting scree-covered line of the Grey Corries appears through the bealach between the two Munros: a notch in the otherwise impenetrable high eastern barrier of the Nevis Range. The rocky summit can feel very bleak and exposed during bad weather, however in settled weather it's a delight. The small summit of Carn Mor Dearg does not have the capacity to hold many people, but fortunately, except for those rare sunny summer days of extreme clarity, it is quite normal to find that you are the only person on the summit and can have it entirely to yourself.

The CMD Arête to Ben Nevis

Descend south along the crest of the granite ridge as it quickly sharpens to form the CMD Arête and the gradient slackens. The CMD Arête is very rocky from the outset and keeping to the crest makes for an exposed but relatively easy scramble in good weather conditions. The solid upstanding blocks of granite offer good grip when dry and exhibit innumerable scratch marks along the entire line of the ridge, etched out during winter conditions when ice axes and crampons are undoubtedly required in order to cling to the crest. Faint discontinuous dirt and scree paths to the east of the crest high above Coire Giubhsachan avoid some of the exposure on the more difficult sections for those that feel inclined; however these paths frequently resurface at the top of the ridge. For those that love a sense of exposure and panoramic views, keeping to the crest is essential.

For a seasoned hill walker or scrambler, the clambering up and down, around and across large solid granite boulders amongst scenery of such magnificence is over a kilometre of pure mountaineering delight. The crest really is one-way traffic and on a busy day (maybe as many as 12 walkers on the long ridge at any one time), you may encounter several fellow scramblers on the ridge, most picking their way along from Carn Mor Dearg towards Ben Nevis, although a lesser number also do the route in reverse.

The rugged crest heads due south then abruptly swings to the SW as it starts to turn majestically around the head of Coire Leis. As it does so, scrambling along the rocky crest becomes easier with a more defined and continuous path along the south-eastern side. The ridge then descends at an easy gradient to a low point (still >1050m altitude), with steep drops abutting the ridge to the right as granite cliffs and crags plunge over 100 metres down the rugged headwall of Coire Leis. Now high above Coire Giubhsachan and the meandering Allt Coire Giubhsachan on one side, your eye turns to look down the length of the perfect hanging U-shaped valley of the Allt a' Mhuilinn, between the steep scree-covered granite slopes of Carn Mor Dearg and the grey andesite cliffs and crags of Ben Nevis' North Face.

Coire Leis comprises some beautifully wild and rugged terrain, becoming increasingly rocky and remote in its upper reaches. A small lochan nestles into the granitic contours more than 100m beneath the sheer walls of the CMD Arête, fed by meltwater streams from residual winter snows well into the summer months. Originating amongst the screes and melting winter snow at the head of Coire Leis, the Allt a' Mhuilinn carves a rough and undulatory course north-westward through initially bouldery then increasingly heathery topography, towards the open and partially-forested valley of the Great Glen. The dark grey brooding cliffs of Ben Nevis rise straight above to the west, becoming ever closer and more imposing as progress is made along the Arête. Vast grey scree slopes radiate from the base of the cliffs along with a vast expanse of grass and moss, testifying to the extremely cold and damp climate in upper Coire Leis. Meanwhile to the south, grassy slopes drop away abruptly to the largely hidden grassy tranquillity of Glen Nevis far below, across the opposite side of which the two Binneins, An Gearanach, Sgurr a' Mhaim and Stob Ban dominate the scene.

As the Arête starts to rise again after the low point, the crest consists of a pile of upturned boulders involving some more committed scrambling to keep to the very top, again over solid blocks of grippy granite. As before, an eroded path contours across the SE side just below the crest, avoiding some of the exposure. A final section of more level scrambling is next, involving the traverse of several short granite rock bridges about 1 metre wide, accompanied by steep drops on both sides. The granite gives good grip, but the crossing of these rock bridges would be unnerving with a strong crosswind.

Suddenly the thin line of the Arête widens and a large well-built cairn marks the point where a line of abseil posts used to lead down into Coire Leis. These were originally constructed in the 1960s by the Kinloss Mountain Rescue Team, but many became unsafe over the years and they were finally removed during the summer of 2012. A sudden change in rock type beneath the feet is easily discernible here, from red granite to dark grey andesite, a finer grained volcanic rock of different chemical composition that comprises the central core of the Ben Nevis Massif.

The final climb north-westward up the andesite boulder field to the summit of Ben Nevis is very steep and unrelenting on tired legs; however this is comfortingly the final section of climbing for the day. From the Ben, it is all downhill and time for the knees to take the strain in addition to the tired muscles. A faint paler scree path zigzags through the boulder field and it is important to not stray to the right of the path, as steep cliffs and crags line the eastern margin of this wide boulder slope. This is indeed a very cold spot, as large iced cornices often persist along the eastern rim of this boulder slope well into July, perched beneath vertical cliffs supporting the vast summit plateau of Ben Nevis.

The summit of the Ben is suddenly reached as the steep gradient abruptly eases off. The huge cairn at the trig point appears, along with ruins of the hotel and observatory, numerous other memorials and probably about 10 times as many people as you have seen on the entire walk so far. Somehow this detracts from the feeling of being on a high mountaintop, and feels more like being at a popular tourist attraction rather than in an area of outstanding natural beauty. Essential photos at the trig point can be taken, then you may move cautiously over to the edges of what appears to be a deceptively vast plateau to admire the views in all directions. Immense snow cornices are often preserved in Gardyloo Gulley well into the summer, which cuts quite far into the summit plateau and precariously close to the main Mountain Track up the mountain. Commonly in June and early July, thick cornices line the entire northern rim of the plateau and overhang it, so care should be taken not to unwittingly step out onto them.

Descending from Ben Nevis
back to North Face car park

The descent involves returning down the Mountain Track to the Halfway Lochan, at an altitude of about 570 metres. Just above the loch, the path cuts beneath an impressive waterfall of the Red Burn, a chance to fill up the water bottles after all of the high altitude ridge walking.

Once down near Halfway Lochan, pick up a well-made path leading due north and parallel with the lochan, bearing left when it splits up ahead, to arrive at the far (northern) end of the loch. From here descend the rough, heathery and largely pathless slopes towards the Allt a' Mhuilinn. Ford the burn, which may be potentially impassable after very heavy rainfall, then clamber up the opposite bank to locate the main outbound path and follow it back north-westward through Leanachan Forest to the North Face car park.

The route up onto Carn Mor Dearg's north ridge from the Allt a' Mhuilinn

198

Ben Nevis and Carn Mor Dearg from the southern slopes of Carn Beag Dearg

Loch Eil and Loch Linnhe from the southern slopes of Carn Beag Dearg

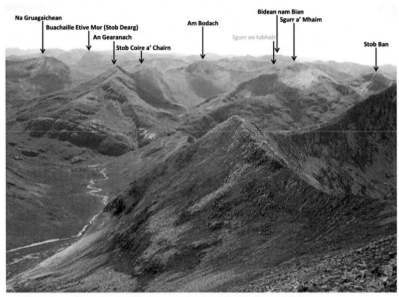

Summer panorama looking south from Carn Mor Dearg

Winter panorama looking south from Carn Mor Dearg

Scrambling along the CMD Arête high above the Allt Coire Giubhsachan

The U-shaped valley of the Allt a' Mhuilinn from the CMD Arête

Looking back along a narrow rock bridge on the CMD Arête to Carn Mor Dearg

Route 14:

Ben Nevis and Carn Mor Dearg via Coire Giubhsachan

This route provides an interesting variant to the "classic" Route 13, starting in attractive Glen Nevis to the south of Ben Nevis and Carn Mor Dearg. The advantages to this route are a traverse of the beautiful Nevis Gorge, Steall Meadows and Coire Giubhsachan, followed by an ascent of Carn Mor Dearg's fine east ridge, less popular but more exhilarating than the standard ascent of the mountain from the north.

This route is ideal for scramblers or those who enjoy traversing narrow rocky ridges, as there is a short section of fairly exposed scrambling at the top of Carn Mor Dearg's east ridge, just beneath the small summit. The main disadvantage is that the start and end points for the walk are more than 8km (5 miles) distant. Therefore, a base in lower Glen Nevis or Fort William and the use of public transport as far as possible into Glen Nevis early in the day is recommended, to avoid an unpleasant long slog back along the road through Glen Nevis to a car parked at the road end. This walk combines Route 6 and Route 13, so these repeated sections are summarised below, and the earlier walk reports should be consulted for a more detailed description.

Ben Nevis and Carn Mor Dearg via Coire Giubhsachan	
Difficulty	Hard
Distance	17.2 km (10.7 miles)
Cumulative ascent	1,370m
Approximate time taken	7-10 hours
Munros	Ben Nevis (1,344m) Carn Mor Dearg (1,220m)
Subsidiary Tops	-
Advisories	• High level of fitness and stamina required • Good head for heights essential • Unsuitable during high winds and on short mid-winter days • Only to be attempted by those with specialist equipment and experience when under snow/ice • Fairly easy but exposed scrambling on the CMD Arête and upper part of Carn Mor Dearg's east ridge • Steep boulderfield ascent onto Ben Nevis • Different start/end points

Route 14 Summary

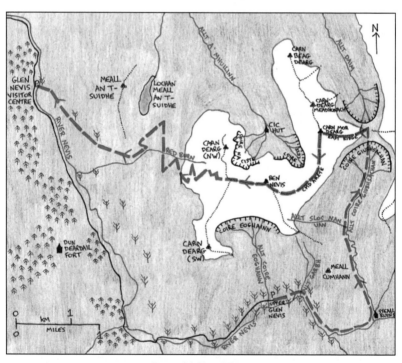

Route 14 Sketch Map

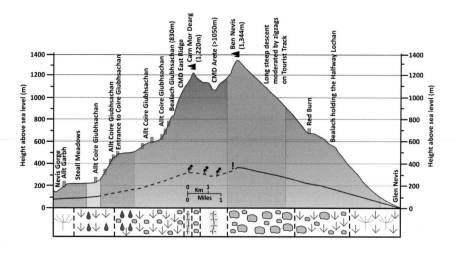

Route 14 Walk Profile

Nevis Gorge to Bealach Giubhsachan (830m)

Start from the popular car park at the road end in Glen Nevis, taking the path heading eastward through the Nevis Gorge to the attractive Steall Meadows, until you reach a bridge fording the Allt Coire Giubhsachan, just before Steall Ruins.

Leave the main path through Glen Nevis just before the bridge and ascend to gain a rough path climbing steeply up the hillside, in close proximity to the Allt Coire Giubhsachan. The entrance to Coire Giubhsachan is abruptly reached as the gradient levels out, with the Allt Coire Giubhsachan meandering attractively across the sub-horizontal boggy gradient.

Traverse up the increasingly wild and remote path to the head of Coire Giubhsachan, crossing numerous streams draining the steep south-eastern slopes of the CMD Arête, before climbing steeply out of Coire Giubhsachan to the bealach at 830m on the left (western) bank of the Allt Coire Giubhsachan. It's worth noting that after you pass the source of the Allt Coire Giubhsachan, no more water is available until halfway down Ben Nevis, when the Red Burn is forded on the Mountain Track, so it is a good idea to fill water bottles here for the exciting high altitude ridge walk ahead. A fine profile of Carn Mor Dearg's east ridge is observed throughout the climb up through Coire Giubhsachan: initially steep, followed by a slackening of the gradient through the middle section, before a final steep and rocky climb to the pointed summit.

The boggy Bealach Giubhsachan, between Carn Mor Dearg and Aonach Mor, comprises a pleasant mixture of several small pools and scattered granite blocks, set amongst lush green grass. This is a fine vantage point to admire the view northward down the bleak U-shaped valley of the Allt Daim, between the north ridge of Carn Mor Dearg and the immense gullied western slopes of Aonach Mor, as well as back southward down much of the length of attractive Coire Giubhsachan.

From the bealach, the exciting ridge-walking starts. The base of Carn Mor Dearg's east ridge rises up steeply to the west, and it is worthwhile locating the steep rough path that climbs in steps up the grassy lower part of the ridge, adjacent to the remains of a crumbling wall.

The east ridge of Carn Mor Dearg to the summit (1220m)

The lower third of Carn Mor Dearg's east ridge is wide but steep, comprising large boulders and smoothed slabs of red granite, offering a few short sections of easy scrambling. The broken path becomes indistinct in places as it twists around the large granite boulders. Above and to the west, the pyramidal summit of Carn Mor

Dearg comes into view, along with the neighbouring summit and jagged east ridge of Carn Dearg Meadhonach (1179m); the latter forming an imposing feature against the skyline, high above the valley of the Allt Daim. The immense bulk of the Aonach Mor-Aonach Beag ridge fills the view to the east, whilst to the south the Allt Coire Giubhsachan meanders away peacefully towards the grassy levels of Glen Nevis, above which rise the dramatic summits of the central and eastern Mamores.

Continue on up the crest of the ridge, which attractively narrows as the slope gradient eases off, with easy walking on a pleasant mixture of solid granite and patchy grass beneath the feet. This really is a fine situation, now high above the meandering Allt Coire Giubhsachan and the rounded summit of Meall Cumhann, all of the Mamores stand proud with the exception of Binnein Beag and Sgurr Eilde Mor, hidden behind Aonach Beag's SW ridge. The summit of Carn Mor Dearg becomes ever closer as you contour along the southern rim of a remote corrie, blanketed in red granite scree derived from cliffs supporting the pointed summit high above. The rubbly granite crest of the CMD Arête pops into view, beyond which the mighty grey cliffs and crags of Ben Nevis' North Face start to appear.

The final climb to the summit of Carn Mor Dearg is steep and comprises the first major scramble of the day, up a fairly narrow and rocky granite ridge, although a small dirt path along the southern side bypasses much of this exposure. The mossy granite blocks along the ridge crest can be quite slippery when wet, so care should be taken through this section. The first feel of exposure is evident but there should be no difficulty if time and care are taken. This would likely be a far different (and notably more dangerous) undertaking in winter conditions or high winds however. Suddenly the summit cairn appears at the top of the rocky ridge, the ridge is steep right up to the summit cairn.

In good weather, the summit of Carn Mor Dearg is perhaps the finest vantage point for the magnificent North Face of Ben Nevis and the spectacular CMD Arête, which links the two mountains. The summit is also a great viewpoint for the Mamore Range from the north, with all summits visible except for Mullach nan Coirean, hidden behind the bulk of Ben Nevis. It is quite common to have the small summit entirely to yourself, in contrast to neighbouring Ben Nevis where the ant-like figures of countless proud walkers can often be picked out, swarming across the extensive summit plateau and peering enquiringly over the cliffs and corries of the mountain's North Face.

The Carn Mor Dearg (CMD) Arête (>1050m) to Ben Nevis (1344m)

Descend south along a sharpening ridge crest to the start of the CMD Arête. Keeping to the rocky crest of the CMD Arête makes for an exposed but fairly easy scramble, although a rough path along the eastern and south-eastern slopes avoids some of the exposure for the faint-hearted. After over a kilometre of scrambling, including the traverse of several short rock bridges about a metre wide, the line of the CMD Arête abruptly widens at a large, well-built cairn, marking the base of a steep boulder field rising to the summit plateau of the Ben. Climb steeply north-westward up the andesite boulder field to the summit of Ben Nevis on a faint path, steering clear of steep cliffs and crags lining the eastern margin of this wide boulder slope.

The summit of Britain's highest mountain is suddenly reached as the slope gradient abruptly eases off. The huge cairn at the trig point appears, along with all the other unnecessary anthropogenic paraphernalia, and probably about 10 times as many people as you have seen on the entire walk so far. Essential photos at the trig point can be taken, then move cautiously over to the edges of what appears to be a deceptively vast plateau, to admire the views in all directions. Vast cornices often line and overhang the northern and eastern rims of the plateau into early summer, and should therefore be carefully avoided by walkers.

Descent from Ben Nevis on the Mountain Track

Descent is via the Mountain Track, the standard route up Ben Nevis in the company of tens, even hundreds, of others. Once down at Halfway Lochan, the main Mountain Track swings sharply to the left to descend the steep southern and western slopes of Meall an t-Suidhe, arriving at the Glen Nevis Visitor Centre or Youth Hostel and including the chance for a refreshing pint at the Ben Nevis Inn. From the visitor centre, there is a walk of about 2.6km (1.6 miles) back into the centre of Fort William along the main road.

The upper section of Carn Mor Dearg's east ridge, with the CMD Arête and cloud-covered Ben Nevis behind

Route 15:

The Ring of Steall

One of the "classics" of the area, the Ring of Steall provides a fine day of high altitude ridge walking across 4 Munro summits and a further 2 Munro Tops. Once up onto the first Munro (An Gearanach), the ridge route never drops below the 850m contour until the final descent off Sgurr a' Mhaim, saving the highest till last. This route forms a superb circuit enclosing the attractive Coire a' Mhail, at the foot of which issues the spectacular Steall Waterfall, which gives the walk its name. A good head for heights is essential and there are several sections of fairly exposed scrambling, as well as some steep ascents and descents on scree.

To many, the Devil's Ridge does not live up to its name, being more of an exposed walk rather than a scramble along most of its length. The most exposed section of scrambling is actually around the rocky Munro Top of An Garbhanach, during the early part of the walk. As with other routes in the area, the most exposed areas of scrambling can usually be circumvented by small paths on the less steep side of the ridge crest. Pick a nice day for this one, to enjoy a scenic day out on one of the most popular ridge routes in the Mamores.

The Ring of Steall	
Difficulty	Hard
Distance	14.7 km (9.1 miles)
Cumulative ascent	1,830m
Approximate time taken	7-10 hours
Munros	Sgurr a' Mhaim (1,099m)
	Am Bodach (1,032m)
	An Gearanach (982m)
	Stob Coire a' Chairn (981m)
Subsidiary Tops	Sgurr an Iubhair (1,001m)
	An Garbhanach (975m)
Advisories	• High level of fitness and stamina required
	• Good head for heights essential
	• Unsuitable during high winds and on short mid-winter days
	• Only to be attempted by those with specialist equipment and experience when under snow/ice
	• Some sections of exposed scrambling, but can be partially circumvented
	• A number of steep ascents and descents on slippery scree

Route 15 Summary

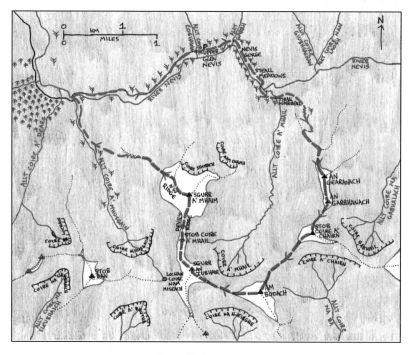

Route 15 Sketch Map

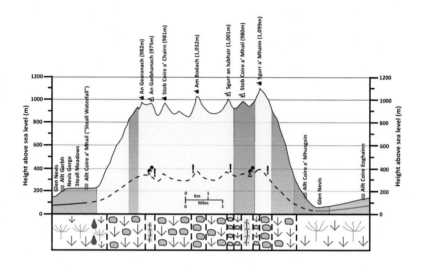

Route 15 Walk Profile

Nevis Gorge to An Gearanach (982m)

Starting from the car park at the road end in Glen Nevis, take the path heading eastward through the impressive Nevis Gorge to the pleasant Steall Meadows. Numerous streams are crossed through the first section of the gorge and it is advisable to make sure the bottles are well filled here, as the majority of the day will be spent in high altitude ridge walking.

Cross the River Nevis via the wire bridge, or just upstream using a series of rocks as stepping stones, then continue past the Steall Hut to the base of the awe-inspiring Steall Waterfall. The Allt Coire a' Mhail (Steall Waterfall River) must be forded next and this can be tricky. Below the crashing foaming waters of the Steall Waterfall are numerous angular blocks of slippery wet schist, around which the water tumbles and cascades. With care, the dry rocks can be used as stepping stones, but it is advisable to avoid those that are wet or mossy. Once the river has been safely crossed, locate a path on the opposite side which continues eastward beneath the steep wooded lower slopes of An Gearanach. The path soon fizzles out in a diffuse area of bog, where waterproof boots are essential to keep the feet dry, however by keeping to the edge of the steep wooded slopes of An Gearanach it is possible to bypass the worst of the soggy ground.

To the east of the boggy area rises a large grassy cone, representing a vegetated ancient scree landslip derived from higher up the northern slopes of An Gearanach. Ascend SE up the relatively steep grassy slopes of this avalanched material, where a small stalker's path can soon be located and followed upward. Higher up this path has been obliterated by a more recent landslide, however by continuing up the western rim of the landslip, the path soon re-emerges again and heads off to the west. The narrow but obvious path, composed of rubbly quartzite and schist, now commences a series of tight zigzags up the steep northern slopes of An Gearanach.

Height is soon gained above Steall Meadows, with the Steall Waterfall now obscured from view by a solid wall of schist. The immense bulks of Ben Nevis, Carn Mor Dearg and Aonach Beag emerge to the north across the opposite side of Glen Nevis, with an attractive view up the valley of the Allt Coire Giubhsachan higher up. The small pointed summit of An Gearanach is obscured throughout the long steep ascent of the mountain's northern face and the apparent summit directly above is in fact a false summit. The summit cairn on An Gearanach sits a little back to the south, the highest point on a ridge that constitutes one of several northern spurs protruding from the main E-W trending Mamore Ridgeline.

The path appears to be ascending towards a sheer cliff that looks impassable from beneath, however before the base of the cliff is reached the small path abruptly angles to the right (west) and then to the left (east), clinging to the steep grassy hillside high above the open valley of upper Glen Nevis. The path, now rather indistinct, rises steeply up a relatively wide grassy ridge to attain the northern end of the An Gearanach-An Garbhanach ridge, with Sgurr an Iubhair, the Devil's Ridge and Sgurr a' Mhaim appearing for the first time across the opposite side of Coire a' Mhail. The tiny pointed summit of An Gearanach suddenly pokes into view ahead to the south, once the northern end of the summit ridge is attained. By this time the views have opened up to the east with the blunt cone of Binnein Beag, summit ridge of Binnein Mor and pointed summits of Na Gruagaichean looking magnificent. A final ascent leads to the small quartzite cairn at the exposed summit of An Gearanach (982m).

The small summit of An Gearanach is a fine viewpoint for the tantalising prospect of the remaining walk ahead. A narrow ridge composed of a pleasant contrast of grey schistose boulders, rubble and green grass descends away southward, narrows, then gently rises to the rocky Munro Top of An Garbhanach (975m). Beyond An Garbhanach there's a steep descent to a narrow bealach, before a climb up grass- and scree-covered slopes to the rounded summit of Stob Coire a' Chairn (981m), situated on the main E-W-trending Mamore Ridgeline. The Mamore Ridgeline undulates westward to reach the base of imposing steep slopes guarded by scree shoots and crags that rise to the rocky summit of Am Bodach (1032m), before curving round the head of Coire a' Mhail on a gentler gradient to the flat-topped summit of Sgurr an Iubhair (1001m). From here another spur strikes out northward from the main Mamore Ridgeline, initially comprising the grassy knife-like Devil's Ridge rising to a high point on Stob Coire a' Mhail. This narrow ridge then descends in undulatory fashion to a rocky low point before rising steeply to the immense quartzite bulk of Sgurr a' Mhaim (1099m), the second highest in the range but the highest peak of the day.

Onto An Garbhanach (975m) and Stob Coire a' Chairn (981m)

Descend southward from An Gearanach on a small path along the narrowing and exposed ridge crest, with very steep grassy and boulder-strewn slopes falling away on both sides. It is easy to see how walkers can mistakenly descend into Coire a' Mhail and then follow the river back towards Glen Nevis during times of bad weather or falling light, as there is no indication that the river is suddenly about to plunge several hundred metres over a sheer rock face as the Steall Waterfall at the foot of the corrie. Fatalities have occurred here, so if it's necessary to descend quickly, do so via the outbound route.

The rise onto An Garbhanach represents the first scramble of the day over solid blocks of schist and quartzite. The scramble along the crest is relatively easy initially, with the upstanding blocks of schist offering good grip in the dry, but a small path winds along the left (eastern) side avoiding some of the exposure. The exposed rocky summit of An Garbhanach is guarded on the right (western) side by precipitous rock faces plunging into Coire a' Mhail, so care should be taken during a traverse of the summit.

The trickiest section is during the steep initial descent from An Garbhanach towards the bealach with Stob Coire a' Chairn, as the small path winds along or close to the crest of the ridge across loose and slippery scree with steep drops to either side. Further down, the ridge descends steeply via a series of large upturned boulders, requiring a rather committed scramble to keep to the crest. Fortunately the slippery scree path winds to the left (eastern) side through this section, circumventing much of the exposure. The narrow bealach is suddenly reached at the base of the steep ridge, with a return to the pleasant mix of grass and scattered blocks of schist beneath the feet.

The ascent up onto Stob Coire a' Chairn and the main Mamore Ridgeline is fairly short but steep on a mixture of schist and patchy grass, becoming rocky at the summit. The summit is spectacularly perched at the head of Coire a' Chairn, with a fine view southward down the U-shaped valley of the Allt Coire na Ba to Kinlochleven, beyond which Buachaille Etive Mor and Glencoe Mountain rise up impressively. There is also a fine view to the north and west from the western margin of the rounded summit, where the source of the Allt Coire a' Mhail in the heads of remote corries between the summits of Am Bodach, Sgurr an Iubhair and Sgurr a' Mhaim can be seen. The Allt Coire a' Mhail meanders attractively like a writhing snake across a gentle lush green grassy gradient towards the foot of the corrie, beyond which the steep southern slopes of Meall Cumhann and Carn Dearg rise up to the immense bulk of the Ben Nevis Massif. The white slash of the Allt Coire Eoghainn cascades down smoothed surfaces of polished granite, from high up the southern slopes of Ben Nevis to Glen Nevis far below. The fine rocky spur out to An Garbhanach and An Gearanach looks impressive close at hand to the north, whilst a stalker's path angles off east across grassy slopes towards the exciting twin summits of Na Gruagaichean and its NW Munro Top. The narrow curving quartzite east ridge of Stob Ban appears through the col between Sgurr an Iubhair and Stob Coire a' Mhail on the Devil's Ridge.

On to Am Bodach (1032m) and Sgurr an Iubhair (1001m)

Descend westward from Stob Coire a' Chairn on a faint path along the fairly wide grassy crest of the ridge, with relatively gentle slopes into the head of Coire a' Mhail to the right (north) and comparatively steeper slopes into the head of Coire a' Chairn to the left (south). The ridge crosses a subsidiary grassy bump before a further small descent leads to the base of Am Bodach's eastern face, adorned by numerous crags and scree. The ascent of Am Bodach, the second highest on the walk, is long and very steep with a few short sections of exposed scrambling and the scree having an annoying tendency to move under the feet. The forced two steps forward and one step back mentality, as the scree slides uncontrollably downslope under the relentless force of gravity, can instil a sense of frustration on the ascent to the summit.

The rocky summit of Am Bodach (1032m) is a revelation and represents a fine viewpoint for the remainder of this magnificent walk. An asymmetrical grassy ridge descends away from the summit, curves around the head of Coire a' Mhail then rises to the flat-topped summit of Sgurr an Iubhair. Aprons of scree cascade down the steeper northern side of the ridge towards the remote head of the corrie. To the left of Sgurr an Iubhair, the final two summits of the western Mamores on the main Mamore Ridgeline appear; Stob Ban and Mullach nan Coirean. The grassy Devil's Ridge protrudes north to connect with the quartzite bulk of Sgurr a' Mhaim, a final steep climb leading to the pointed summit.

Descend from Am Bodach on a narrow rocky path, now high above the longitudinal water body of Loch Leven, before ascending Sgurr an Iubhair (1001m) on a fairly easy gradient, a welcome respite following the steep climb up Am Bodach. Sgurr an Iubhair has had an interesting history in the Munro Tables. The mountain was promoted to Munro status by the Scottish Mountaineering Club in 1981 before being demoted again in 1997, as during the second revision it was considered to have a re-ascent from Am Bodach and Sgurr a' Mhaim that was too small to allow it to be considered a separate mountain. Therefore in the current standing, Sgurr an Iubhair is considered a Munro Top like An Garbhanach. The flat-topped summit of Sgurr an Iubhair offers an awesome view across the tantalising prospect of the Devil's Ridge to Sgurr a' Mhaim, whilst the eastern face of Stob Ban also looks impressive to the west.

The Devil's Ridge to Sgurr a' Mhaim (1099m)

Descend NW from Sgurr an Iubhair on a narrow path to reach a grassy col and the start of the exciting Devil's Ridge. The northern slopes of Sgurr an Iubhair are convex in nature and covered in slippery pale quartzite scree, with the slope gradient initially fairly gentle but becoming steep above the grassy bealach. From the col, Stob Coire a' Mhail rises up directly above, with Sgurr a' Mhaim even higher in the background. A small path meanders its way up the initially wide and grassy ridge towards Stob Coire a' Mhail, while another path descends steeply westward via a series of tight zigzags towards Lochan Coire nam Miseach and the col with Stob Ban. This latter path can be used to ambitiously link the Ring of Steall with the two western Mamores (see alternatives).

The path onto the Devil's Ridge initially winds up the gentle western limb before migrating over towards the increasingly narrow grassy crest as the summit of Stob Coire a' Mhail is approached (980m). It is easy to believe that the name "Devil's Ridge" is a bit of a misnomer until after Stob Coire a' Mhail is traversed. Beyond the summit of this Munro Top, the ridge significantly narrows and a path leads along the top of a knife-like crest, mainly grassy but intermittently rocky and composed predominantly of schist, with steep drops to the right (east) into Coire a' Mhail and to the left (west) into Coire a' Mhusgain. The ridge descends in irregular fashion at a moderate gradient from Stob Coire a' Mhail, with a narrow path to follow and a good head for heights is essential. Albeit a little vertigo-inducing, traversing the crest of the Devil's Ridge presents few other problems during settled weather in summer. However this situation would be completely turned on its head during high or gusty winds, and is suitable only for an elite group of well-equipped and highly experienced winter mountaineers when coated in snow or ice.

The most difficult part is at the first of the two low points on the ridge, where the crest is composed of a series of angular upstanding blocks of schist requiring a rather committed scramble to cross, as there are steep drops to either side. However small paths descend a little and traverse this section on both the eastern and western slopes, avoiding much of the exposure, although there is a short scramble to get back up onto the crest of the ridge. Following a small rise, a second descent with a short section of scrambling across ledges of schist is made to another low point on the ridge, this time grassy in nature, followed by a very steep ascent onto the final grassy section of the Devil's Ridge. The ridge widens significantly as the final increasingly steep climb is made towards Sgurr a' Mhaim, initially grassy in nature but with the upper slopes becoming increasingly blanketed in the infamous white quartzite scree. The large quartzite cairn at the summit of Sgurr a' Mhaim is suddenly reached as the slope gradient abruptly eases off (1099m).

The roughly triangular summit plateau of Sgurr a' Mhaim offers an awesome view northwards to the bulky forms of Ben Nevis, Aonach Mor, Aonach Beag and the pyramidal red granite spire of Carn Mor Dearg, as well as into the head of attractive Coire Giubhsachan and Bealach Giubhsachan connecting Carn Mor Dearg with Aonach Mor. There is an equally fine view southward across the tortuous crest of the grassy Devil's Ridge, the flat-topped summit of Sgurr an Iubhair and the pointed summit of Am Bodach to the Glencoe mountains and northern Blackmount, a complex tangle of peaks sprawling out towards the horizon. The central-eastern Mamores with their summit ridges, pointed summits and vast expanses of quartzite and schistose scree look fine to the east, with the pointed volcano-like peak of Schiehallion visible on a clear day, poking up behind Binnein Mor's South Top. The open view to the west takes in the lower contrasting summits of Stob Ban and Mullach nan Coirean, beyond which lie the shimmering waters of Loch Linnhe.

The descent from Sgurr a' Mhaim is long, steep and unpleasant, via its NW ridge. Contour around the head of Coire Sgorach, the distinctive and conspicuous corrie on the mountain's northern face, to pick up a path which initially descends fairly steeply through slippery and loose quartzite blocks and scree. Lower down, the ridge becomes grassy but steepens further, finally terminating above a rough path heading into Coire a' Mhusgain. Turn right here and follow the path back to the road just north of the Lower Falls car park, then follow the road eastward for just over 2km back to the car park at the road end.

Alternatives

For the super-fit, the ambitious, or those not content with just doing the "standard" Ring of Steall, this route could be extended to include the two western Mamores along the Mamore Ridgeline, Stob Ban and Mullach nan Coirean. This would approximately add an extra 8km (5 miles) distance and 500m of ascent to the statistics for the Ring of Steall route given above.

Head back southward along the Devil's Ridge from Sgurr a' Mhaim to reach the bealach below Sgurr an Iubhair. Veer off to the right (west) from the bealach to locate a small rubbly path, which descends steeply via a series of tight zigzags towards the north-western outflow at the foot of the roughly circular Lochan Coire nam Miseach. Continue west to pick up a stalker's path running along the northern side of the Mamore Ridgeline, across the high bealach between Sgurr an Iubhair and Stob Ban, to intersect **Route 10 – The Stob Ban and Mullach nan Coirean Circuit**. From here follow the trail outlined under **Route 10**, ascending Stob Ban via its east ridge before traversing the easy ridge encircling Coire Dheirg to Mullach nan Coirean, then descending via the Mullach's NE Ridge back to Achriabhach in Glen Nevis.

The Devil's Ridge and Sgurr a' Mhaim from Sgurr an Iubhair

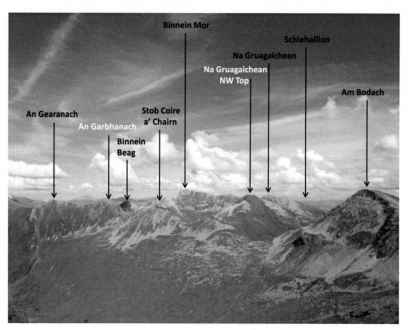

Panorama looking east from Sgurr an Iubhair

The Devil's Ridge to Sgurr a' Mhaim from Stob Coire a' Mhail

Looking back to the rocky low point on the Devil's Ridge,
with Stob Coire a' Mhail behind

Panorama looking south from Sgurr a' Mhaim

The Nevis Range from Sgurr a' Mhaim

Route 16:

The Eastern Mamores

The four Munros at the eastern end of the Mamore Range are more remote and comparatively poorly frequented, being further from Fort William and popular Ben Nevis. However, a hike into these mountains rewards the walker with some of the most spectacular views and exciting ridges as well as solitude. Binnein Mor is indeed the highest in the range, with a stupendous 360° panoramic view from its bouldery summit ridge. These mountains have been carved out of the ancient metamorphic Dalradian bedrock, with vast expanses of pale white quartzite scree and stark rocky outcrops adding to their attractive appeal.

The best bases from which to walk into these eastern mountains are Kinlochleven or Mamore Lodge, where the mountains can be easily accessed from the south via a number of good stalker's paths and Land Rover tracks. Alternatively, with a little more effort, these fine peaks can be reached from the car park at the road end in Glen Nevis, by continuing eastward along the path from there through the spectacular Nevis Gorge and Steall Meadows into upper Glen Nevis. These mountains can easily be arranged into different groupings, depending on the

fitness and stamina of the group and the weather conditions, with a couple of shorter alternatives suggested at the end of this section.

The Eastern Mamores	
Difficulty	Very Hard
Distance	19.9 km (12.4 miles)
Cumulative ascent	1,771m
Approximate time taken	8-11 hours
Munros	Binnein Mor (1,130m) Na Gruagaichean (1,056m) Sgurr Eilde Mor (1,010m) Binnein Beag (943m)
Subsidiary Tops	Binnein Mor South Top (1,062m) Na Gruagaichean NW Top (1,041m)
Advisories	• Very high level of fitness and stamina required • A good height for heights is essential • Unsuitable during high winds and on short winter days • Only to be attempted by those with specialist equipment and experience when under snow/ice • A number of steep ascents/descents on slippery scree • Some short sections of easy scrambling • These mountains can be spread over a couple of days via a number of alternative shorter routes

Route 16 Summary

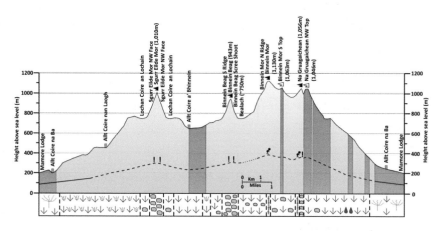

Route 16 Walk Profile

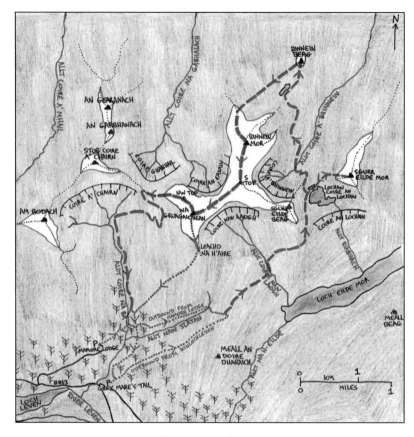

Route 16 Sketch Map

Starting from Mamore Lodge

This route is best started from Mamore Lodge, which is located at about 200m altitude, removing some of the early climb. However at the time of writing, this lodge had closed down and it is uncertain if it will still be possible to park here in the future. There is also a small layby just off the B863 at the end of the tarmac road to Mamore Lodge, with space for a few cars but involving a 1.5km (0.9 mile) walk and 180m climb to arrive at the lodge.

From Mamore Lodge, take the small path bypassing to the south of the stalker's cottage to rejoin a wide well-made track, which starts to curve north-eastward around the south-eastern slopes of Am Bodach. A short distance (roughly 0.2km, 0.1 miles) after the stalker's cottage, before the path turns round to the north, vacate the main track and take a small stony path leading off to the right (east). This path descends to cross the Allt Coire na Ba on a wooden bridge, a river lined with scattered silver birch trees and representing a chance to fill up the water bottles. Climb up the opposite bank and follow the stony path as it crosses another small path (the descent route back to Kinlochleven), before ascending to join a large well-made Land Rover track contouring along the lower southern slopes of Na Gruagaichean. Follow this track eastward on a gentle gradient for just over a kilometre until it is joined by a path from the south, representing the route up from Kinlochleven.

Starting from Kinlochleven

Starting from the Grey Mare's Tail Waterfall car park in the north of the town, take the path starting between the car park and the white church of St. Paul's Kinlochleven. This path is known as the Ciaran Path and dates back to Victorian times. There is a complex network of small stalker's paths along the western slopes of Meall an Doire Dharaich, not all of which are marked on some detailed topographic maps of the area, so it is important to follow the correct directions to intersect the Land Rover track up from Mamore Lodge.

The path reaches a junction just behind the church and car park. Turn left here on a well-made path signposted for the "Grey Mares Waterfall", then almost immediately veer off right onto a rougher and rockier path, which higher up is signposted "Loch Eilde Mor Path". This path can also be reached from the well-made path towards the Grey Mares Tail Waterfall, however be careful to follow the sign towards Loch Eilde Mor and avoid descending towards the waterfall. Alternatively one could descend for a fantastic view of what must be one of the most impressive waterfalls in Scotland: A huge column of foaming and roaring white water formed as the Allt Coire na Ba plummets down a rugged wall of quartzite, appearing very much like a grey horse's tail, hence its name. This fine waterfall is without doubt Kinlochleven's version of Glen Nevis' Steall Waterfall but is somewhat more easily accessible, being only a few minutes' walk from the car park.

After a short section uphill, the path splits again, with the rounded summit of Meall an Doire Dharaich in view straight ahead. Take the left path, flanked by silver birch trees on the left, aiming to the left of Meall an Doire Dharaich's summit. The path soon splits again up ahead, where the left-hand option should again be taken, to cross a small stream and climb up the opposite bank. The path splits one final time up ahead; however in this case both paths coalesce higher up. For simplicity it is probably easiest to take the left option and climb very steeply up a western spur off Meall an Doire Dharaich. From here the route becomes much simpler, following the rough rocky path as it climbs steeply through deciduous forest, composed predominantly of silver birch, beech and oak. The path forms multiple strands, anastomosing across the steep spur much like the fluvial channels in a braided river system. The Allt a' Chumhainn crashes through a dramatic narrow forested gorge on the left hand side, bordered by extremely steep slopes. If the Grey Mare's Tail Waterfall is Kinlochleven's answer to Glen Nevis' Steall Waterfall, then this valley of the Allt a' Chumhainn must be considered as Kinlochleven's equivalent of the Nevis Gorge. A river on the right side also flows through an impressive narrow gorge, and at one point both gorges converge to form a narrower section along the spur.

Higher up, the path emerges from open birch forest onto the heathery and grassy mountainside, contouring along the undulating northern slopes of Meall an Doire Dharaich and rising at a gentler gradient to a high point. This open section allows fantastic views up the head of Coire a' Chairn to the high summits of Am Bodach, Stob Coire a' Chairn and Na Gruagaichean, enclosing the attractive corrie. After the high point, the path descends gently towards the Land Rover track up from Mamore Lodge, crossing several small streams before climbing to gain the track. The onward route up to the steep southern slopes of Sgurr Eilde Beag becomes obvious during this descent.

Ascending to Coire an Lochain and onto Sgurr Eilde Mor (1010m)

Just to the west of where the Kinlochleven path joins the main track from Mamore Lodge, leave this track and take a smaller path which starts to climb north-eastward across the lower south-eastern slopes of Na Gruagaichean. This track soon crosses the Allt Coire nan Laogh, which drains from a high corrie enclosed by the summits of Na Gruagaichean, Binnein Mor's South Top and Sgurr Eilde Beag, representing an ideal place to fill up with water. Shortly after this river is forded, the path starts to climb more steeply as it rounds the southern slopes of Sgurr Eilde Beag, clinging to the steep heathery slopes high above the large water body of Loch Eilde Mor, before splitting into two options. Instead of taking the left fork up the steep southern slopes to the summit of Sgurr Eilde Beag (**Route 16a**), take the right path, which after a further short climb, levels out onto the broad and remote saddle called Coire an Lochain. This bealach supports a large loch (Lochan Coire an Lochain), filling the irregular contours in a fantastic location between the high summits of Sgurr Eilde Beag and Sgurr Eilde Mor. A pleasant mixture of grass, heather and scattered blocks of quartzite and schist surrounds the loch, which represents a fine spot for a paddle in the icy cold waters on a hot day.

The path enters Coire an Lochain at the base of the steep eastern slopes of Sgurr Eilde Beag, with the white quartzite east face of Binnein Mor filling the view to the NW, the summit appearing as a sharp white quartzite point, largely obscuring the short level summit ridge beyond. The fine east ridge of the mountain is well defined against the skyline, however the easier north ridge used for ascent on this route is hidden behind the immense bulk of the mountain. To the north, white quartzite screes rising to the rounded conical summit of Binnein Beag fill the middle ground, with the broad southern ridge of the mountain well defined. Beyond Binnein Beag, the many grey scree-covered summits of the Grey Corries, Stob an Cul Choire, Sgurr a' Bhuic and Stob Coire Bhealaich comprise the backdrop.

Across the loch to the east, heathery and grassy slopes, partially blanketed by vast rivulets and fans of grey quartzite screes, rise to the rounded summit of Sgurr Eilde Mor, with ridges radiating off to the right (south ridge), left (west ridge) and behind the summit (NE ridge). Any one of these can provide a route to the summit of the mountain. The most technically easy from this side is to contour northward round the western margin of Lochan Coire an Lochain to pick up a small path along the northern bank, leading eastward across a grassy sill between the main large loch in Coire an Lochain and a smaller subsidiary loch to the north. This path starts up over grass and scattered quartzite slabs on the lower slopes of Sgurr Eilde Mor's west ridge, before traversing a little to the east and ascending the steep scree-covered NW face of the mountain. The path becomes increasingly steep upward, and the scree is very slippery underfoot in the upper section. The apparent summit visible directly above during much of the ascent is in fact a false summit (a common occurrence in the Scottish Highlands), and the summit cairn is actually hidden behind the bulk of the mountain until the path levels out near the top of the west ridge. There's a fine aerial view of Lochan Coire an Lochain from the point where the path intersects the west ridge of the mountain, the tranquil waters attractively filling in the irregular topography of the bealach and reflecting the colour of the sky. Turn left (east) here for a short easy walk along the upper section of the west ridge to the summit cairn on Sgurr Eilde Mor (1010m).

Sgurr Eilde Mor without doubt feels like the most remote of the Mamores, being somewhat isolated from the other mountains in the range and with a great sense of openness, especially to the north, south and east. The open view to the north takes in the huge, bulky forms of the Nevis Range and the sprawling scree-covered ridges of the Grey Corries, over the small cone of Binnein Beag and the high bealach with Binnein Mor. To the west, Sgurr Eilde Beag and Binnein Mor are prominent, a fine ridge rising in punctuated fashion from the former to the vast bulk of the latter, fully asserting itself as the tallest in the range. The rocky summit of Na Gruagaichean and adjacent level grassy ridge of its NW Munro Top appear through the col between Binnein Mor and Sgurr Eilde Beag. To the south, the summits and ridges of the northern Blackmount, Buachaille Etive Mor, Buachaille Etive Beag and Bidean nam Bian form a fine backdrop, rising high above the hidden valley of Glencoe which conveniently conceals the busy A82.

The route to Binnein Beag (943m)

As a direct consequence of its isolation, there is a bit of a walk from here to reach the next Munro, Binnein Beag, inevitably involving a fairly significant descent of almost 400m into the head of Coire a' Bhinnein. Head back down the west ridge until the top of the rough path down the NW face is located. Descend via the ascent route, initially taking care down the steep slippery screes, to reach the base of Sgurr Eilde Mor's west ridge. Follow the path back westward across the sill at the head of Lochan Coire an Lochain, after which the path starts to climb up the western slopes of Sgurr Eilde Beag. Just after the point where this path starts to ascend, a small stony path hairpins off to the right, initially descending NE then quickly turning north-westward to descend into the spectacular Coire a' Bhinnein, between the massive bulks of Binnein Mor and Sgurr Eilde Mor. Soon the infant Allt Coire a' Bhinnein is easily forded, before the good stalker's path gradually rises along the eastern slopes of Binnein Mor on the west side of the corrie. The path emerges at the south-eastern rim of a broad bealach between Binnein Beag and Binnein Mor, adjacent to a fairly small lochan filling a prominent depression. The wide scree-covered southern ridge of Binnein Beag is visible throughout this section of the walk, curving up from the broad bealach with Binnein Mor to the rounded summit. Turn NE and follow a faint path, above and roughly parallel to the lochan, to arrive at the base of Binnein Beag's south ridge. The broken path threads its way up steeply through sharp white quartzite scree and boulders, involving a few short sections of easy scrambling, to abruptly arrive at the rounded summit of Binnein Beag (943m). A low enclosing quartzite wall has been built at the summit, open to the south, which when seated could provide some protection from bitter northerly, easterly or westerly winds that frequently ravage the exposed summit.

The summit of Binnein Beag represents a fine viewpoint for the Nevis Range, with the south-eastern peaks of Sgurr a' Bhuic, Stob Coire Bhealaich and Aonach Beag fairly close at hand to the NW, across the wide open valley of upper Glen Nevis. Initially rising from the pointed quartzite Munro Top of Sgurr a' Bhuic, the grassy ridge curves up to the pointed summit of Stob Coire Bhealaich, before rising to the large rounded bulk of Aonach Beag. The grassy convex SW ridge of this mountain is well seen from here, curving away from the summit, initially at a gentle gradient, before steepening and plunging into the open grassy meadows of upper Glen Nevis. In contrast, the cold craggy eastern face of the mountain falls away precipitously into a hidden valley, thick snow wedges suspended in high corries. The broad grassy southern slopes of Aonach Mor loom up behind, remote glacially-scoured corries on the eastern face holding snow long into the warm summer months. The shapely red pointed summit of Carn Mor Dearg pierces into the sky above Aonach Beag's SW ridge, with the spectacular Carn Mor Dearg Arête curving gracefully round to merge with a vast grey boulder field beneath the south-eastern slopes of Ben Nevis. The Grey Corries poke up to the north and north-east, steep grassy lower slopes rising to a complex tangle of grey scree-covered ridges and sharp pointed summits. Binnein Mor looks impressive to the west, its grassy north ridge standing out against the skyline, ascending and merging with the rather rougher and rockier NE and E ridges to support the short nearly level summit ridge. From this eastern vantage point, the Binnein Mor Massif takes on the appearance of a large ridge tent.

Behind, the two northern spurs off the main Mamore Ridge terminating at An Gearanach and Sgurr a' Mhaim look fine, along with the rounded summits of Stob Coire a' Chairn, Sgurr an Iubhair and the rugged east face of Am Bodach. Directly beneath and to the west lies the broad open grassy valley of upper Glen Nevis, down the centre of which the River Nevis cuts an angular course through the solid metamorphic bedrock. The rounded scree-covered summits of Sgurr Eilde Mor and Sgurr Eilde Beag rise above the remote head of Coire a' Bhinnein and the watery wastes of Coire an Lochain to the south, with Glencoe Mountain and Buachaille Etive Mor appearing in the background through the saddle.

On to Binnein Mor (1130m) and Na Gruagaichean (1056m)

There are two options for the descent back to the boggy bealach with Binnein Mor. The easiest option is back down the south ridge of the mountain, but the most direct route is to descend a steep scree shoot down the south-western face, which can vary from exciting to terrifying depending on one's love or hate of scree. The slope is very steep and the scree very liable to move under the feet. The confident and experienced can quickly bounce/skid down the scree, whilst for those with poor balance, holding onto more stable pieces of rock to either side is advisable. The angular quartzite blocks are very sharp and may shorten the life of your walking boots by a few years, with a fall onto them best avoided at all costs. The scree shoot terminates just above the broad boggy bealach between the Binneins, on the opposite side of the large loch reached earlier during the ascent out of Coire a' Bhinnein.

Continue south-west across the fairly level ground of the bealach, before starting to rise towards the base of Binnein Mor's grassy north ridge. From here it is possible to either contour round west to reach the steep base of the north ridge, or take a more direct route and ascend very steep grassy slopes WSW, to attain the ridge somewhat higher up. The asymmetrical but fairly wide north ridge, falling away steeply to the left (east) in the upper section, consists of a pleasant mixture of grass and scattered quartzite blocks, curving gracefully up to the fairly level summit ridge of Binnein Mor. The climb up to the highest summit in the Mamore Range from the bealach is long, steep and tough but is the last major climb of the day, the final summit Na Gruagaichean being 74m lower. The north ridge rises high above a couple of remote lochans perched in a high corrie enclosed by Binnein Mor's north and north-east ridges, the final section becoming increasingly rocky as the summit ridge is approached. A short scramble along the level summit ridge, across or around large angular blocks of quartzite, leads to the small rocky summit of Binnein Mor at its southern end. This small summit, the highest in the Mamores, offers one of the best panoramas in the range.

The Binnein Mor Massif strikes out northwards as the easternmost of three northern spurs off the main E-W trending Mamore Ridgeline, almost the entire length of which can be seen from Binnein Mor's rocky summit. This ridgeline follows a twisting and undulatory course over a further 5 Munros, 5 Munro Tops and two different rock types to terminate at the rounded grassy granite ridges of Mullach nan Coirean and Meall a' Chaorainn, high above Loch Linnhe and some 10km (6.2 miles) distant (as the crow flies). From Binnein Mor, the attractive ridgeline, composed of a pleasant mixture of green grass and patchy grey scree, descends due south then rises to the small bump comprising Binnein Mor's South Top. From here the ridge swings abruptly south-westward to connect with the pointed white rocky quartzite summit of Na Gruagaichean, curving round the head of north-facing Coire an Easain. Adjacent to Na Gruagaichean, a narrow col bordered by steep slopes separates the Munro from the level grassy ridge of its NW Top, beyond which the main grassy crest of the Mamore Ridgeline falls away to a bealach, before rising to the rounded rocky bump of Stob Coire a' Chairn. The second spur radiates out to the north from here, initially sharply descending to a high bealach, before rising over the narrow rocky crest of An Garbhanach to the pointed Munro summit of An Gearanach at its northern end, high above Glen Nevis.

The main Mamore Ridgeline descends from Stob Coire a' Chairn over a minor bump before rising very steeply to the rocky summit of Am Bodach, whose craggy east face looks imposing even from this distant location. A gentle descent and ascent leads to the rounded summit of Sgurr an Iubhair, a former Munro but demoted during a 1997 revision of the Munro Tables by the Scottish

Mountaineering Club. From there the third and westernmost spur punches north, rising over the sharpening grassy crest of the Devil's Ridge to Stob Coire a' Mhail, descending in irregular fashion to a low point, before rising up the immense quartzite bulk of Sgurr a' Mhaim. This mountain is the second highest in the range, dominating the view from lower Glen Nevis with its attractive glacially-sculpted northern corrie (Coire Sgorach). The Mamore Ridgeline then abruptly descends out of view, before curving up the narrow quartzite east ridge of Stob Ban, appearing through the bealach between Sgurr an Iubhair and Stob Coire a' Mhail. The rounded grassy ridges of Mullach nan Coirean at the western termination of the Mamore Ridgeline appear through the bealach between Stob Coire a' Mhail and Sgurr a' Mhaim.

By contrast, the view to the east is much more open, falling away down the rubbly crest of the mountain's east ridge to the rounded rocky summit of Sgurr Eilde Mor, grey screes taking on a strong brown tinge in the upper section and already looking some distance away. Beyond and to the south lie the large Blackwater Reservoir and the open boggy expanse of Rannoch Moor. The Grey Corries rise up beyond the conical peak of Binnein Beag, which appears low, insignificant and hardly worthy of Munro status from this much higher vantage point. The Nevis Range dominates the view across the opposite side of Glen Nevis to the north, with the grey rounded andesite bulk of Ben Nevis and grassy schistose mass of Aonach Beag contrasting starkly with the delicate pointed red summits of Carn Mor Dearg and Carn Dearg Meadhonach in between. There is a fine view up the glacially scoured U-shaped valley of the Allt Coire Giubhsachan until it curves away north-eastward behind the bulk of Aonach Beag, with the stream issuing from the centre of the valley and tumbling in a series of foaming cascades southward into Glen Nevis.

After taking time to savour this magnificent panorama, gradually descend easily on the well-defined broad ridgeline southward across a mixture of grass and quartzite boulders, before gently ascending to reach the Binnein's South Top (1062m). From here, an easy descent can be made on a wide ridge to Sgurr Eilde Beag and then down the mountain's steep southern slopes, to reach the main track back to Kinlochleven and Mamore Lodge. Given sufficient time and light however, the inclusion of Na Gruagaichean requires comparatively little effort from here. Follow the narrowing ridgeline south-westward as it descends to a low point, before rising up to the summit of Na Gruagaichean (1056m). The quartzite ridge turns increasingly rocky and asymmetrical towards the summit, falling away steeply to the north in a series of steep scree slopes and small crags, involving a scramble to keep to the rocky crest. A well-defined small path runs parallel to the ridgeline on the grassy southern side, avoiding much of the exposure.

The small rocky summit of Na Gruagaichean is another fine viewpoint, especially looking westward along almost the entire length of the longitudinal water body of Loch Leven, past the vast craggy east face of Am Bodach, the Pap of Glencoe and Beinn na Caillich, to catch a glimpse of the distant Loch Linnhe. Binnein Mor also looks impressive, it's ridge tent-like appearance now viewed from the opposite direction, as opposed to from the summit of Binnein Beag earlier in the day. The Mamore Ridgeline to the east is composed of an attractive mixture of bright green grass and grey scree, organised into distinct NE-SW trending bands, reflecting the structural grain of the underlying bedrock. This structure is a throwback to the Caledonian Orogeny and formation of the metamorphic core of the Mamore Range under extreme heat and pressure around 480-430 million years ago. The somewhat distant rounded summit of Sgurr Eilde Mor, bathed in scree, pokes up through the bealach between Sgurr Eilde Beag and Binnein Mor's South Top.

From Na Gruagaichean, two descent options are possible. The easiest involves descending along the mountain's south ridge to

Leachd na h-Aire, then turning south-westward and vacating the ridge to descend pathless heathery slopes, steep in places. This route intersects a well-made Land Rover track along the lower reaches of Coire a' Chairn, which can be followed back to Mamore Lodge or Kinlochleven. This is probably the best (and potentially only) option during snow or ice cover, deteriorating weather conditions or falling light. The second option, described below, continues along the Mamore Ridgeline to include an ascent of the level grassy ridge comprising Na Gruagaichean's NW Top, before descending via the head of Coire a' Chairn back to Mamore Lodge or Kinlochleven.

Ascending Na Gruagaichean's NW Top (1041m) and descent back to Mamore Lodge or Kinlochleven

The grassy summit ridge of Na Gruagaichean's NW Top lies very close by to the NW, but the route between them involves descending very steeply on scree to a tight enclosed bealach between the two mountains. This is the shortest scree descent of the day, but involves steep drops to the west and north into the heads of Coire a' Chairn and Coire an Easain respectively, so care should be taken to avoid a slip here. This section is extremely dangerous when covered in snow or ice and should not be attempted under those conditions. Once negotiated, a short steep ascent leads up to the level grassy ridge of the NW Top and the final summit of the day (1041m). From here, the main crest of the Mamore Ridgeline descends over a mixture of grass and patchy quartzite scree to a bealach, before grassy slopes rise to the next Munro, Stob Coire a' Chairn.

Follow the crest of the ridge as it descends and just as the bealach is reached, a small path darts off left (south), to start the descent into Coire a' Chairn and then on back towards Kinlochleven via a series of zigzags. This path is visible during the lower part of the descent from Na Gruagaichean's NW Top. At first the path almost doubles back and contours along the south-western slopes of Na Gruagaichean's NW Top, even involving a little ascent, before turning back to the NW and then W, to descend across peaty and boggy terrain into the head of Coire a' Chairn. The path should then be followed as it descends southward on the left (east) bank of the Allt Coire na Ba through grassy and intermittently boggy terrain, where the path tends to fizzle out or becomes indistinct. Always keep on the east bank of the river and with a little searching around, the path will appear further downstream. Just after some ruins and a small building with a corrugated iron roof, the path widens into a track and forks just before a bridge across the Allt Coire na Ba. To head back to Mamore Lodge, take the right fork and cross this bridge to follow the well-made track southward then south-westward back to the car park. To return to Kinlochleven, take the left fork, then after about 130m turn off on a small path to the right (south) through thick ferns. Follow this path as it descends due south then south-west, lower down passing the Grey Mare's Tail Waterfall, to arrive back at the Grey Mare's Tail car park in the north of the town.

Alternatives

This long circuit can be broken down into a couple of shorter alternatives over two days, to spend more time in these attractive mountains. The two suggested routes (P.240 and 241) are perhaps among the most popular.

Route 16a: Binnein Mor and Na Gruagaichean

Starting from Mamore Lodge or Kinlochleven, follow the route as described above until the path contours up the southern slopes of Sgurr Eilde Beag. Where the path forks before emerging at the bealach holding Lochan Coire an Lochain, veer off left on a small path which climbs steeply up the southern slopes of Sgurr Eilde Beag to the summit (980m). The summit of this Munro Top is the easternmost on the E-W trending Mamore Ridgeline, offering fine views eastward across Coire an Lochain to Sgurr Eilde Mor.

Follow the relatively wide asymmetrical ridge WNW, taking care of steep drops to the right (NE). The ridge descends a little over quartzite scree to a low point, then climbs at a moderate gradient across patchy grass, quartzite and schistose scree to reach Binnein Mor's South Top (1062m). From here follow the well-defined fairly broad spur northward to reach the level summit ridge of Binnein Mor, with the summit at the southern end (1130m). Return back southward to Binnein Mor's South Top, then traverse the narrowing ridgeline south-westward, as it descends to a low point then rises to the rocky quartzite summit of Na Gruagaichean, involving some scrambling near the summit. Descend from Na Gruagaichean as described above, either down the mountain's south ridge or by continuing to the mountain's NW Top and descending through Coire a' Chairn.

Route 16b: Binnein Beag and Sgurr Eilde Mor

Starting from Mamore Lodge or Kinlochleven, follow the route as described above until Coire an Lochain. Instead of taking the path towards Sgurr Eilde Mor along the northern margin of the main loch, descend into Coire a' Bhinnein, then ascend to the bealach between the Binneins, in order to climb the more distant Munro Binnein Beag first. Ascend Binnein Beag via its south ridge, then return via the same route to the northern part of Coire an Lochain. Cross the grassy sill along the northern margin of the main loch in Coire an Lochain and ascend Sgurr Eilde Mor as described above, via its NW face. Return via the same route to Coire an Lochain, then descend via the outbound route back to Mamore Lodge or Kinlochleven.

The Grey Mare's Tail Waterfall

241

Loch Leven from the southern slopes of Na Gruagaichean

Sgurr Eilde Mor from the northern bank of Lochan Coire an Lochain

Descending the scree shoot down Binnein Beag towards Binnein Mor

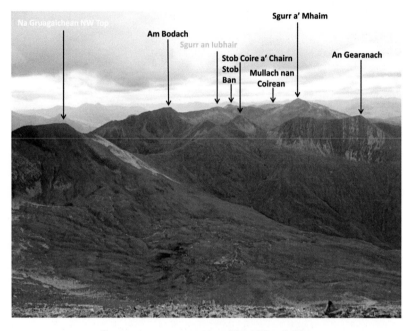

Summer panorama westward from Binnein Mor

Winter panorama westward from Binnein Mor

244

Summer panorama looking south from Binnein Mor to Na Gruagaichean

Winter panorama looking south from Binnein Mor to Na Gruagaichean

Binnein Mor from Na Gruagaichean, with Sgurr Eilde Mor beyond

Summer panorama looking west down the length of Loch Leven from Na Gruagaichean

Route 17:

The Nevis Range Challenge

The mother of all walks in the Nevis Range, this trek links all of the Munros and a number of the other Munro Tops to provide a fantastic but strenuous long day of mountain walking, hard to beat anywhere else in the British Isles. Once onto the first Munro, Aonach Beag, you will not drop beneath the 830m contour (barely below Munro level) until descending off the final and highest Munro of the day, Ben Nevis. A very high degree of fitness and stamina are required, with a good head for heights essential for the traverse of Carn Mor Dearg's narrow east ridge, and the spectacular Carn Mor Dearg (CMD) Arête. This route links two of the walks already described in this book (Route 12 and Route 14), and is summarised in this section below. For a more detailed description of the route and scenery, please refer to the earlier individual walk reports.

The Nevis Range Challenge	
Difficulty	Very Hard
Distance	20.9 km (13 miles)
Cumulative ascent	2,010m
Approximate time taken	8-11 hours
Munros	Ben Nevis (1,344m)
	Aonach Beag (1,234m)
	Aonach Mor (1,221m)
	Carn Mor Dearg (1,220m)
Subsidiary Tops	Stob Coire Bhealaich (1,101m)
	Sgurr a' Bhuic (963m)
Advisories	• Very high level of fitness and stamina required
	• Good head for heights essential
	• Unsuitable during high winds and on short winter days
	• Only to be attempted by those with specialist equipment and experience when under snow/ice
	• Very steep descent on heavily eroded path and scree off Aonach Mor
	• Fairly easy but exposed scrambling on the CMD Arête and upper part of Carn Mor Dearg's east ridge
	• Steep boulderfield ascent onto Ben Nevis
	• Different start/end points

Route 17 Summary

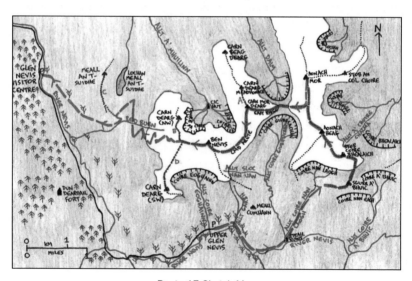

Route 17 Sketch Map

248

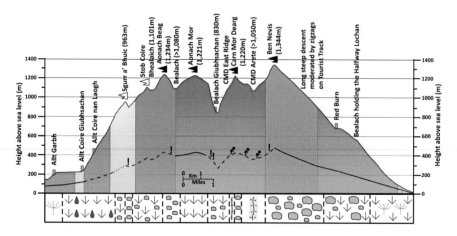

Route 17 Walk Profile

Nevis Gorge to Aonach Mor (1221m)

Take the rocky path leading eastward from the popular car park at the road end in Glen Nevis. The path leads initially through the tight confines of the Nevis Gorge and then into the broad expanse of the Steall Meadows, until a wooden bridge fording the Allt Coire Giubhsachan is reached, with the Steall Ruins immediately beyond.

From the Steall Ruins, leave the main path through Glen Nevis and ascend a small path towards the NE, rising parallel and on the right (east) bank of the Allt Coire nan Laogh. The path ascends close to the river for some distance, then starts to climb high above it, eventually becoming indistinct as it rounds the western grassy slopes of Sgurr a' Bhuic's western Top. Contour round to the northern side of the Top and ascend to gain the crest of a broad rubbly ridge, which rises to the small pointed summit of Sgurr a' Bhuic (963m) at its eastern end.

Descend northwards from the summit on an eroded scree path to a low point above Coire nan Laogh, then locate a small path which climbs NNE to gain the ridge to Stob Coire Bhealaich. The

249

ridge swings abruptly left (west) to reach the small rocky summit of the Munro Top (1101m). Follow the ridge westward until the path descends a little then climbs towards the NW, parallel to the precipitous eastern face, to reach the bleak rounded summit of Aonach Beag (1234m).

From Aonach Beag, descend the convex slope north-westward on a scree path, keeping clear of precipitous drops to the east, to reach the bealach with Aonach Mor. From here, follow the dirt path up an easy gradient to the summit cairn in the centre of the wide grassy ridge (1221m).

Descending from Aonach Mor (1221m) and onto Carn Mor Dearg (1220m)

Retrace your steps from the summit cairn back southward on the path along the centre of the summit ridge. However, about a third of the way down, veer off right (west) on a faint grassy path, which heads towards and then runs roughly parallel with the western rim. The path descends gently to reach a small granite cairn marking the top of a rough spur, which must be descended to reach the bealach with Carn Mor Dearg (Bealach Giubhsachan). Descend the very steep spur with care and caution, down an eroded path consisting of slippery granite rubble and scree, to abruptly reach the grassy Bealach Giubhsachan at its base (830m).

From the bealach, ascend the east ridge of Carn Mor Dearg, initially on a steep path adjacent to a crumbling wall. The ridge is broad and steep at the base, narrowing attractively as the gradient slackens through the middle section before you reach a steep rocky final section to the small summit cairn, involving some relatively easy but exposed scrambling (1220m). This scrambling can largely be circumvented via a small path on the southern side of the crest.

Traversing the CMD Arête to Ben Nevis (1344m)

Descend south along a narrowing ridge to reach the start of the CMD Arête. Keep to the rocky crest for some fairly easy but exposed scrambling, or descend to take discontinuous paths which contour across the eastern (left) side, avoiding some of the exposure. As the ridge crest turns abruptly south-west to round the headwall of Coire Leis and descends to a low point (>1050m), scrambling along the rocky crest becomes easier with a better defined and more continuous path along the south-eastern side. As the ridge begins to rise again, more committed scrambling is required to keep to the crest; however eroded paths on the south-east (left) side once again avoid the worst of the exposure. This is followed by a more level section of scrambling, including the traverse of several short rock bridges about 1m wide, to arrive at a large cairn marking the base of a massive boulder slope and an abrupt widening of the ridge. Ascend the steep boulder slope on a broken path, steering clear of precipitous cliffs on the right (east) side, to arrive at the broad summit plateau on Ben Nevis (1344m).

Descend Ben Nevis via the Mountain Track, initially down the steep western slopes of the mountain to Halfway Lochan, followed by the southern then western slopes of Meall an t-Suidhe to the Glen Nevis Visitor Centre or Youth Hostel.

Alternatives

For the super fit, some of the other exciting Tops within the Nevis Range were missed out on the above route, and additional detours can be made to include them. These are:

■ **Option A: Carn Dearg Meadhonach (1179m)** – easily included by following the broad ridgeline northward from Carn Mor Dearg. This will add an extra 1.1km (0.7 miles) distance and about 70m of ascent to return to Carn Mor Dearg. This ridge offers fantastic views of the cliffs, crags and corries of Ben Nevis' North Face throughout, and is a nice inclusion in good weather.

■ **Option B: Carn Dearg (1221m, Ben Nevis' NW Munro Top)** - easily traversed by following the northern rim of Ben Nevis' summit plateau. This route allows fine views east and north to the attractive red pointed summits along Carn Mor Dearg's north ridge, with the vast slopes of Aonach Mor and Aonach Beag beyond.

■ **Option C: Meall an t-Suidhe (711m)** – traversed by continuing a little further down the Mountain Track from Lochan Meall an t-Suidhe, then turning off NW at the apex of the first zigzag to climb the southern Top of Meall an t-Suidhe. Follow the broad ridgeline northward, as it descends to a narrow col then climbs to reach the summit cairn. This would approximately add an extra 2.2km (1.4 miles) distance and 170m of ascent to return to the Mountain Track, but allows fine views west to Loch Linnhe and Loch Eil.

■ **Option D: Carn Dearg (1220m, Ben Nevis' SW Munro Top)** – traversed with significantly more effort by taking the left variant of the Mountain Track on the descent from Ben Nevis. This path veers off south-westward across a ridge between Coire Eoghainn and Five Finger Gulley to reach the Munro Top, adding an extra 2.5km (1.6 miles) and 250m of ascent to return to the Mountain Track. This route is suitable only in clear weather under summer conditions, when this ridge can be safely and easily navigated.

Recommended websites

Useful internet resources offering practical advice and further information about the Scottish Munros include:

www.walkhighlands.co.uk

www.outdoorcapital.co.uk

www.munromap.co.uk

www.munromagic.com

www.smc.org.uk

Some of these sites offer web-based forums, where fellow walkers can share their experiences and find out more about a route or climb they are planning to attempt.